ANNIHILATION OF CASTE

B.R. AMBEDKAR

PEACOCK BOOKS

Published by
PEACOCK BOOKS
7/22, Ansari Road, Darya Ganj, New Delhi-110002
Phones : +91-11-40775252, 40775214, 23273880, 23275880
Fax : +91-11-23285873
Web : www.atlanticbooks.com
E-mail : orders@atlanticbooks.com

Peacock Books is an imprint of
Atlantic Publishers and Distributors (P) Ltd

First Published 1936

Printed & bound in India by Atlantic Print Services

Dr. B.R. Ambedkar (1891–1956) was a visionary leader, social reformer and the principal architect of the Indian Constitution. Born into an untouchable family in Mhow, Madhya Pradesh, Ambedkar faced discrimination and social ostracism from a young age, which fueled his lifelong commitment to social justice and equality. Despite facing immense obstacles, he earned multiple degrees, including a Doctorate in Law from the London School of Economics and Columbia University. He became a leading figure in India's fight against caste-based discrimination. As an intellectual and activist, Ambedkar dedicated his life to challenging the deeply entrenched caste system and advocating for the rights of the oppressed, particularly Dalits. His most famous work, *Annihilation of Caste*, is a scathing critique of the caste system and the social structures perpetuating inequality. Ambedkar calls for completely dismantling caste-based hierarchies in this groundbreaking text and stresses the importance of social reform, education and political empowerment for marginalised communities. Dr. Ambedkar's contributions to Indian society and politics are monumental, and his ideas continue to inspire movements for social justice and equality. His legacy as a champion of human rights and social reform remains profound and enduring.

Noteworthy works by Dr. B.R. Ambedkar:

- *The Problem of the Rupee (1923)*
- *Annihilation of Caste (1944)*
- *Thoughts on Linguistic States (1955)*
- *The Buddha and His Dhamma (1957)*

CONTENTS

INTRODUCTION TO THE TEXT

Annihilation of Caste is a cornerstone of the Dalit movement and a touchstone for debates about caste and social justice in India. In this powerful work, Ambedkar exposes the cruelty and absurdity of caste-based oppression and calls for the annihilation of caste as a precondition for the creation of a truly democratic and egalitarian society.

Varnashrama dharma, also known as *chaturvarna,* is the caste system in Hinduism that divides society into four varnas based on the hereditary occupation of each caste. These four varnas are Brahmins, Kshatriyas, Vaishyas, and Shudras. The Brahmins are the Vedic scholars and priests; the Kshatriyas are warriors and administrators; the Vaishyas are the farmers and servants; and lastly, the Shudras are servants and labourers. However, there exists a fifth category of people who are not part of the varna systems because of their sins. They are known as the "untouchables" and are ostracised from society. Today, the term "untouchable" has been replaced with the Marathi term "Dalit" (Broken People), which is also used to refer to the "Scheduled Caste."

Ambedkar was born into this category. As a result, he and his family were treated as outcasts throughout his childhood. As Ambedkar grew up, he realised how the varna system is more of a social model designed specifically to benefit the privileged upper caste and advocated for the abolition of the varna system throughout his life.

The Jat-Pat Todak Mandal of Lahore, a Hindu reformist organisation that had invited Ambedkar to give its annual lecture in 1936, requested and received the speech's text in advance and found the contents "unbearable". The Mandal withdrew its invitation after realising that Ambedkar meant to use the event as a platform to condemn both Hinduism and the practice of caste. Ambedkar himself paid for the printing of 1,500 copies of the speech's text in May 1936. Six languages were shortly added to the translation.

The text has been studied by scholars, writers, and thinkers for years now. Although he could not deliver his speech, Ambedkar made sure that he got an opportunity to speak his truth. He was determined not to be silenced. When the Jat-Pat Todak Mandal refused to let Ambedkar give his speech at the conference, little did they know that they were igniting a fire that would eventually weaken the iron hold of the caste system in India.

Although this speech was highly criticised by everyone, one criticism stood out, and that was of M.K. Gandhi. While Ambedkar deemed the injustice of the caste system a political matter, which called for a political resolution for the advancement of the untouchables, Gandhi perceived the caste issue as a complex social challenge and aimed to counter it through a transformative shift in the perception of people towards the untouchables. Therefore, he began to refer to them as "Harijans", which means children of God. Gandhi stood for a sort of revamping of the caste system with no hierarchies.

Hence, it becomes imperative to also take into consideration the political context of the time to understand the varying perspectives of both reformers. Both had their own set of ideals and a huge number of supporters.

The Annihilation of Caste is an important text in the repertoire of social texts in India and reading it will help the reader to not only understand the injustice of the caste system but how there exists a bias against the marginalised community that seeps into our daily conversations. Reading Ambedkar's writings will help the readers to close the knowledge gap between what the majority of Indians believe the caste system to be and what it really is.

ANNIHILATION OF CASTE

"Know truth as truth and untruth as untruth."

—Buddha

"He that will not reason is a bigot. He that cannot reason is a fool. He that dare not reason is a slave."

—H. Drummond

PREFACE TO THE SECOND EDITION, 1937

The speech prepared by me for the Jat-Pat Todak Mandal of Lahore has had an astonishingly warm reception from the Hindu public for whom it was primarily intended. The English edition of one thousand five hundred copies was exhausted within two months of its publication. It has been translated into Gujarati and Tamil. It is being translated into Marathi, Hindi, Punjabi and Malayalam. The demand for the English text still continues unabated. To satisfy this demand it has become necessary to issue a second edition. Considerations of history and effectiveness of appeal have led me to retain the original form of the essay—namely, the speech form—although I was asked to recast it in the form of a direct narrative.

To this edition I have added two appendices. I have collected in Appendix I the two articles written by Mr Gandhi by way of review of my speech in the *Harijan*, and his letter to Mr Sant Ram, a member of the Jat-Pat Todak Mandal.

In Appendix II, I have printed my views in reply to the articles of Mr Gandhi collected in Appendix I. Besides Mr Gandhi, many others have adversely criticised my views as expressed in my speech. But I have felt that in taking notice of such adverse comments, I should limit myself to Mr Gandhi. This I have done not because what he has said is so weighty as to deserve a reply, but because to many a Hindu he is an oracle, so great that when he opens his lips it is expected that the argument must close and no dog must bark.

But the world owes much to rebels who would dare to argue in the face of the pontiff and insist that he is not infallible. I do not care for the credit which every progressive society must give to its rebels. I shall be satisfied if I make the Hindus realise that they are the sick men of India, and that their sickness is causing danger to the health and happiness of other Indians.

B.R. AMBEDKAR

PREFACE TO THE THIRD EDITION, 1944

The second edition of this essay appeared in 1937, and was exhausted within a very short period. A new edition has been in demand for a long time. It was my intention to recast the essay so as to incorporate into it another essay of mine called "Castes in India: Their Mechanism, Genesis and Development," which appeared in the issue of the *Indian Antiquary* journal for May 1917. But as I could not find time, and as there is very little prospect of my being able to do so, and as the demand for it from the public is very insistent, I am content to let this be a mere reprint of the second edition.

I am glad to find that this essay has become so popular, and I hope that it will serve the purpose for which it was intended.

B.R. AMBEDKAR
22, Prithviraj Road
New Delhi
1 December 1944

PROLOGUE

On 12 December 1935, I received the following letter from Mr Sant Ram, the secretary of the Jat-Pat Todak Mandal:

> My dear Doctor Saheb,
>
> Many thanks for your kind letter of the 5th December. I have released it for press without your permission for which I beg your pardon, as I saw no harm in giving it publicity. You are a great thinker, and it is my well-considered opinion that none else has studied the problem of caste so deeply as you have. I have always benefited myself and our Mandal from your ideas. I have explained and preached it in the *Kranti* many times and I have even lectured on it in many conferences. I am now very anxious to read the exposition of your new formula—"It is not possible to break caste without annihilating the religious notions on which it, the caste system, is founded." Please do explain it at length at your earliest convenience, so that we may take up the idea and emphasise it from press and platform. At present, it is not fully clear to me.
>
> Our executive committee persists in having you as our president for our annual conference. We can change our dates to accommodate your convenience. Independent Harijans of Punjab are very much desirous to meet you and discuss with you their plans. So, if you kindly accept our request and come to Lahore to preside over the conference it will serve double purpose. We will invite Harijan leaders of all shades of opinion and you will get an opportunity of giving your ideas to them.

The Mandal has deputed our assistant secretary, Mr Indra Singh, to meet you at Bombay in Xmas and discuss with you the whole situation with a view to persuade you to please accept our request.

* * * * * *

The Jat-Pat Todak Mandal is, I was given to understand, an organisation of caste-Hindu social reformers, with the one and only aim, namely, to eradicate the caste system from amongst the Hindus. As a rule, I do not like to take any part in a movement which is carried on by caste Hindus. Their attitude towards social reform is so different from mine that I have found it difficult to pull on with them. Indeed, I find their company quite uncongenial to me on account of our differences of opinion. Therefore, when the Mandal first approached me, I declined their invitation to preside. The Mandal, however, would not take a refusal from me, and sent down one of its members to Bombay to press me to accept the invitation. In the end I agreed to preside. The annual conference was to be held at Lahore, the headquarters of the Mandal. The conference was to meet at Easter, but was subsequently postponed to the middle of May 1936.

The reception committee of the Mandal has now cancelled the conference. The notice of cancellation came long after my presidential address had been printed. The copies of this address are now lying with me. As I did not get an opportunity to deliver the address from the presidential chair, the public has not had an opportunity to know my views on the problems created by the caste system. To let the public know them, and also to dispose of the printed copies which are lying on my hand, I have decided to put the printed copies of the address in the market. The accompanying pages contain the text of that address.

The public will be curious to know what led to the cancellation of my appointment as the president of the conference. At the start, a dispute arose over the printing of the address. I desired that the address should be printed in Bombay. The Mandal wished that it should be printed in Lahore, on the grounds of economy. I did not agree, and insisted upon having it printed in Bombay. Instead of their agreeing to my proposition, I received a letter signed by several members of the Mandal, from which I give the following extract:

27 March 1936 Revered

Doctor ji,

Your letter of the 24th instant addressed to Sjt. Sant Ram has been shown to us. We were a little disappointed to read it. Perhaps you are not fully aware of the situation that has arisen here. Almost all the Hindus in the Punjab are against your being invited to this province. The Jat-Pat Todak Mandal has been subjected to the bitterest criticism and has received censorious rebuke from all quarters. All the Hindu leaders among whom being Bhai Parmanand, MLA (ex-president, Hindu Mahasabha), Mahatma Hans Raj, Dr Gokal Chand Narang, minister for local self-government, Raja Narendra Nath, MLC etc., have dissociated themselves from this step of the Mandal.

Despite all this the runners of the Jat-Pat Todak Mandal (the leading figure being Sjt. Sant Ram) are determined to wade through thick and thin but would not give up the idea of your presidentship. The Mandal has earned a bad name.

Under the circumstances it becomes your duty to cooperate with the Mandal. On the one hand, they are being put to so much trouble and hardship by the Hindus, and if on the other hand you too augment their difficulties it will be a most sad coincidence of bad luck for them.

We hope you will think over the matter and do what is good for us all.

* * * * * *

This letter puzzled me greatly. I could not understand why the Mandal should displease me, for the sake of a few rupees, in the matter of printing the address. Secondly, I could not believe that men like Sir Gokal Chand Narang had really resigned as a protest against my selection as president, because I had received the following letter from Sir Gokal Chand himself:

5, Montgomery Road, Lahore

7 February 1936

Dear Doctor Ambedkar,

I am glad to learn from the workers of the Jat-Pat Todak Mandal that you have agreed to preside at their next anniversary to be held at Lahore during the Easter holidays. It will give me much pleasure if you stay with me while you are at Lahore.

More when we meet.

Yours sincerely,

G.C. Narang

******

Whatever be the truth, I did not yield to this pressure. But even when the Mandal found that I was insisting upon having my address printed in Bombay, instead of agreeing to my proposal the Mandal sent me a wire that they were sending Mr Har Bhagwan to Bombay to "talk over matters personally". Mr Har Bhagwan came to Bombay on the 9th of April. When I met Mr Har Bhagwan, I found that he had nothing to say regarding the issue. Indeed, he was so unconcerned regarding the printing of the address—whether it should be printed in Bombay or in Lahore—that he did not even mention it in the course of our conversation.

All that he was anxious for was to know the contents of the address. I was then convinced that in getting the address printed in Lahore, the main object of the Mandal was not to save money but to get at the contents of the address. I gave him a copy. He did not feel very happy with some parts of it. He returned to Lahore. From Lahore, he wrote to me the following letter:

Lahore, 14 April 1936

My dear Doctor Saheb,

Since my arrival from Bombay, on the 12th, I have been indisposed owing to my having not slept continuously for five or six nights, which were spent in the train. Reaching here I came to know that you had come to Amritsar. O, I would have seen you there if I were well enough to go about. I have made over your address to Mr Sant Ram for translation and he has liked it very much, but he is not sure whether it could be translated by him for printing before the 25th. In any case, it would have a wide publicity and we are sure it would wake the Hindus up from their slumber.

The passage I pointed out to you at Bombay has been read by some of our friends with a little misgiving, and those of us who would like to see the conference terminate without any untoward incident would prefer that at least the word "Veda" be left out for the time being. I leave this to your good sense. I hope, however, in your concluding paragraphs you will make it clear that the views expressed in the address are your own and that the responsibility does not lie on the Mandal. I hope you will not mind this statement of mine and would let us have 1,000 copies of the address, for which we shall, of course, pay.

To this effect I have sent you a telegram today. A cheque of ₹ 100 is enclosed herewith which kindly acknowledge, and send us your bills in due time.

I have called a meeting of the reception committee and shall communicate their decision to you immediately. In the meantime, kindly accept my heartfelt thanks for the kindness shown to me and the great pains taken by you in the preparation of your address. You have really put us under a heavy debt of gratitude.

Yours sincerely,

Har Bhagwan

PS.: Kindly send the copies of the address by passenger train as soon as it is printed, so that copies may be sent to the press for publication.

Accordingly, I handed over my manuscript to the printer with an order to print thousand copies. Eight days later, I received another letter from Mr Har Bhagwan which I reproduce below:

Lahore, 22 April 1936

Dear Dr Ambedkar,

We are in receipt of your telegram and letter, for which kindly accept our thanks. In accordance with your desire, we have again postponed our conference, but feel that it would have been much better to have it on the 25th and 26th, as the weather is growing warmer and warmer every day in the Punjab. In the middle of May it would be fairly hot, and the sittings in the daytime would not be very pleasant and comfortable. However, we shall try our best to do all we can to make things as comfortable as possible, if it is held in the middle of May.

There is, however, one thing that we have been compelled to bring to your kind attention. You will remember that when I pointed out to you the misgivings entertained by some of our people regarding your declaration on the subject of change of religion, you told me that it was undoubtedly outside the scope of the Mandal and that you had no intention to say anything from our platform in that connection. At the same time when the manuscript of your address was handed to me you assured me that that was the main portion of your address and that there were only two or three concluding paragraphs that you wanted to add. On receipt of the second instalment of your address we have been taken by surprise, as that would make it so lengthy, that we are afraid very few people would read the whole of it. Besides that you have more than once stated in your address that you had decided to walk out of the fold of the Hindus and that that was your last address as a Hindu. You have also unnecessarily attacked the morality and reasonableness of the Vedas and other religious books of the Hindus, and have at length dwelt upon the technical side of Hindu religion, which has absolutely no connection with the problem at issue, so much so that some of the passages have become irrelevant and off the point, We would have been very pleased if you had confined your address to that portion given to me, or if an addition was necessary, it would have been limited to what you had written on Brahminism, etc. The last portion which deals with the complete annihilation of the Hindu religion and doubts the morality of the sacred books of the Hindus as well as a hint about your intention to leave the Hindu fold does not seem to me to be relevant.

I would therefore most humbly request you on behalf of the people responsible for the conference to leave out the passages referred to above, and close the address with what was given to me or add a few paragraphs on Brahminism, We doubt the wisdom of making the address unnecessarily provocative and pinching. There are several of us who subscribe to your feelings and would very much want to be under your banner for remodelling the Hindu religion. If you had decided to get together persons of your cult, I can assure you a large number would have joined your army of reformers from the Punjab.

In fact, we thought you would give us a lead in the destruction of the evil of [the] caste system, especially when you have studied the subject so thoroughly, and strengthen our hands by bringing about a revolution and making yourself as a nucleus in the gigantic effort, but [a] declaration of the nature made by you, when repeated, loses its power, and becomes a hackneyed term. Under the circumstances, I would request you to consider the whole matter and make your address more effective by saying that you would be glad to take a leading part in the destruction of the caste system if the Hindus are willing to work in right earnest towards that end, even if they had to forsake their kith and kin and the religious notions. In case you do so, I am sanguine that you would find a ready response from the Punjab in such an endeavour.

I shall be grateful if you will help us at this juncture as we have already undergone much expenditure and have been put to suspense, and let us know by the return of post that you have condescended to limit your address as above. In case you still insist upon the printing of the address *in toto,* we very much regret it would not be possible—rather advisable—for us to hold the conference, and would prefer to postpone it *sine die,* although by doing so we shall be losing the goodwill of the people because of the repeated postponements. We should, however, like to point out that you have carved a niche in our hearts by writing such a wonderful treatise on the caste system, which excels all other treatises so far written and will prove to be a valuable heritage, so to say. We shall be ever indebted to you for the pains taken by you in its preparation.

Thanking you very much for your kindness and with best wishes.

I am yours sincerely,

Har Bhagwan

To this letter I sent the following reply:

27 April 1936

Dear Mr Har Bhagwan,

I am in receipt of your letter of the 22nd April. I note with regret that the reception committee of the Jat-Pat Todak Mandal "would prefer to postpone the conference *sine die*" if I insisted upon printing the address *in toto.* In reply I have to inform you that I also would prefer to have the conference cancelled—I do not like to use vague terms—if the Mandal insisted upon having my address pruned to suit its circumstances. You may not like my decision. But I cannot give up, for the sake of the honour of presiding over the conference, the liberty which every president must have in the preparation of the address. I cannot give up, for the sake of pleasing the Mandal, the duty which every president owes to the conference over which he presides, to give it a lead which he thinks right and proper. The issue is one of principle, and I feel I must do nothing to compromise it in any way.

I would not have entered into any controversy as regards the propriety of the decision taken by the reception committee. But as you have given certain reasons which appear to throw the blame on me, I am bound to answer them. In the first place, I must dispel the notion that the views contained in that part of the address to which objection has been taken by the committee have come to the Mandal as a surprise. Mr Sant Ram, I am sure, will bear me out when I say that in reply to one of his letters I had said that the real method of breaking up the caste system was not to bring about inter-caste dinners and inter-caste marriages but to destroy the religious notions on which caste was founded, and that Mr Sant Ram in return asked me to explain what he said was a novel point of view. It was in response to this invitation from Mr Sant Ram that I thought I ought to elaborate in my address what I had stated in a sentence in my letter to him. You cannot, therefore, say that the views expressed are new. At any rate, they are not new to Mr Sant Ram, who is the moving spirit and the leading light of your Mandal. But I go further and say that I wrote this part of my address not merely because I felt it desirable to do so. I wrote it because I thought that it was absolutely necessary to complete the argument. I am amazed to read that you characterise the portion of the speech to which your committee objects as "irrelevant and off the point". You will allow me to say that I am a lawyer and I know the rules of relevancy as well as any member of your committee. I most emphatically maintain that the portion objected to is not only most relevant but is also most important. It is in that part of the address that I have discussed the ways and means of breaking up the caste system. It may be that the conclusion I have arrived at as to the best method of destroying caste is startling and painful. You are entitled to say that my analysis is wrong. But you cannot say that in an address which deals with the problem of caste it is not open to me to discuss how caste can be destroyed.

Your other complaint relates to the length of the address. I have pleaded guilty to the charge in the address itself. But who is really responsible for this? I fear you have come rather late on the scene. Otherwise you would have known that originally I had planned to write a short address, for my own convenience, as I had neither the time nor the energy to engage myself in the preparation of an elaborate thesis. It was the Mandal which asked me to deal with the subject exhaustively, and it was the Mandal which sent down to me a list of questions relating to the caste system and asked me to answer them in the body of my address, as they were questions which were often raised in the controversy between the Mandal and its opponents, and which the Mandal found difficult to answer satisfactorily. It was in trying to meet the wishes of the Mandal in this respect that the address has grown to the length to which it has. In view of what I have said, I am sure you will agree that the fault respecting the length of the address is not mine.

I did not expect that your Mandal would be so upset because I have spoken of the destruction of the Hindu religion. I thought it was only fools who were afraid of words. But lest there should be any misapprehension in the minds of the people, I have taken great pains to explain what I mean by religion and destruction of religion. I am sure that nobody, on reading my address, could possibly misunderstand me. That your Mandal should have taken a fright at mere words as "destruction of religion, etc.", notwithstanding the explanation that accompanies them, does not raise the Mandal in my estimation. One cannot have any respect or regard for men who take the position of the reformer and then refuse even to see the logical consequences of that position, let alone following them out in action.

You will agree that I have never accepted to be limited in any way in the preparation of my address, and the question as to what the address should or should not contain was never even discussed between myself and the Mandal. I had always taken for granted that I was free to express in the address such views as I held on the subject. Indeed, until you came to Bombay on the 9th April, the Mandal did not know what sort of an address I was preparing. It was when you came to Bombay that I voluntarily told you that I had no desire to use your platform from which to advocate my views regarding change of religion by the Depressed

Classes. I think I have scrupulously kept that promise in the preparation of the address. Beyond a passing reference of an indirect character where I say that "I am sorry I will not be here, etc.", I have said nothing about the subject in my address. When I see you object even to such a passing and so indirect a reference, I feel bound to ask, did you think that in agreeing to preside over your conference I would be agreeing to suspend or to give up my views regarding change of faith by the Depressed Classes? If you did think so, I must tell you that I am in no way responsible for such a mistake on your part. If any of you had even hinted to me that in exchange for the honour you were doing me by electing [me] as president, I was to abjure my faith in my programme of conversion, I would have told you in quite plain terms that I cared more for my faith than for any honour from you.

After your letter of the 14th, this letter of yours comes as a surprise to me. I am sure that anyone who reads them both will feel the same. I cannot account for this sudden volte-face on the part of the reception committee. There is no difference in substance between the rough draft which was before the committee when you wrote your letter of the 14th, and the final draft on which the decision of the committee communicated to me in your letter under reply was taken. You cannot point out a single new idea in the final draft which is not contained in the earlier draft. The ideas are the same. The only difference is that they have been worked out in greater detail in the final draft. If there was anything to object to in the address, you could have said so on the 14th. But you did not. On the contrary, you asked me to print off 1,000 copies, leaving me the liberty to accept or not the verbal changes which you suggested. Accordingly, I got 1,000 copies printed, which are now lying with me. Eight days later you write to say that you object to the address and that if it is not amended the conference will be cancelled. You ought to have known that there was no hope of any alteration being made in the address. I told you when you were in Bombay that I would not alter a comma, that I would not allow any censorship over my address, and that you would have to accept the address as it came from me. I also told you that the responsibility for the views expressed in the address was entirely mine, and if they were not liked by the conference I would not mind at all if the conference passed a resolution condemning them. So anxious was I to relieve your Mandal from having to assume responsibility for my views—and also with the object of not getting myself entangled by too intimate an association with your conference—I suggested to you that I desired to have my address treated as a sort of an inaugural address and not as a presidential address, and that the Mandal should find someone else to preside over the conference and deal with the resolutions. Nobody could have been better placed to take a decision on the 14th than your committee. The committee failed to do that, and in the meantime cost of printing has been incurred which, I am sure, with a little more firmness on the part of your committee, could have been saved.

I feel sure that the views expressed in my address have little to do with the decision of your committee. I have reason to believe that my presence at the Sikh Prachar Conference held at Amritsar has had a good deal to do with the decision of the committee. Nothing else can satisfactorily explain the sudden volte-face shown by the committee between the 14th and the 22nd April. I must not, however, prolong this controversy, and must request you to announce immediately that the session of the conference which was to meet under my presidentship is cancelled. All the grace has by now run out, and I shall not consent to preside, even if your committee agreed to accept my address as it is, *in toto.* I thank you for your appreciation of the pains I have taken in the preparation of the address. I certainly have profited by the labour, if no one else does. My only regret is that I was put to such hard labour at a time when my health was not equal to the strain it has caused.

Yours sincerely,

B.R. Ambedkar

* * * * * *

This correspondence will disclose the reasons which have led to the cancellation by the Mandal of my appointment as president, and the reader will be in a position to lay the blame where it ought properly to belong. This is I believe the first time when the appointment of a president is cancelled by the reception committee because it does not approve of the views of the president. But whether that is so or not, this is certainly the first time in my life to have been invited to preside over a conference of caste Hindus. I am sorry that it has ended in a tragedy. But what can anyone expect from a relationship so tragic as the relationship between the reforming sect of caste Hindus and the self-respecting sect of Untouchables, where the former have no desire to alienate their orthodox fellows, and the latter have no alternative but to insist upon reform being carried out?

B.R. AMBEDKAR

Rajgriha, Dadar

Bombay—14

15 May 1936

ANNIHILATION OF CASTE

An Undelivered Speech, 1936

Friends, I am really sorry for the members of the Jat-Pat Todak Mandal who have so very kindly invited me to preside over this conference. I am sure they will be asked many questions for having selected me as the president. The Mandal will be asked to explain as to why it has imported a man from Bombay to preside over a function which is held in Lahore. I believe the Mandal could easily have found someone better qualified than myself to preside on the occasion. I have criticised the Hindus. I have questioned the authority of the Mahatma whom they revere. They hate me. To them I am a snake in their garden. The Mandal will no doubt be asked by the politically minded Hindus to explain why it has called me to fill this place of honour. It is an act of great daring. I shall not be surprised if some political Hindus regard it as an insult. This selection of mine certainly cannot please the ordinary religiously minded Hindus.

The Mandal may be asked to explain why it has disobeyed the shastric injunction in selecting the president. According to the shastras, the Brahmin is appointed to be the guru for the three varnas. वर्णानाम ब्राह्मणो गुरु: is a direction of the shastras. The Mandal therefore knows from whom a Hindu should take his lessons and from whom he should not. The shastras do not permit a Hindu to accept anyone as his guru merely because he is well versed. This is made very clear by Ramdas, a Brahmin saint from Maharashtra, who is alleged to have inspired Shivaji to establish a Hindu Raj. In his *Dasbodh,* a socio-politico-religious treatise in Marathi verse, Ramdas asks, addressing the Hindus, can we accept an *antyaja* to be our guru because he is a pandit (i.e., learned)? He gives an answer in the negative.

What replies to give to these questions is a matter which I must leave to the Mandal. The Mandal knows best the reasons which led it to travel to Bombay to select a president, to fix upon a man so repugnant to the Hindus, and to descend so low in the scale as to select an antyaja—an Untouchable—to address an audience of the savarnas. As for myself, you will allow me to say that I have accepted the invitation much against my will, and also against the will of many of my fellow Untouchables. I know that the Hindus are sick of me. I know that I am not a *persona grata* with them. Knowing all this, I have deliberately kept myself away from them. I have no desire to inflict myself upon them. I have been giving expression to my views from my own platform. This has already caused a great deal of heartburn and irritation.

I have no desire to ascend the platform of the Hindus, to do within their sight what I have been doing within their hearing. If I am here, it is because of your choice and not because of my wish. Yours is a cause of social reform. That cause has always made an appeal to me, and it is because of this that I felt I ought not to refuse an opportunity of helping the cause—especially when you think that I can help it. Whether what I am going to say today will help you in any way to solve the problem you are grappling with, is for you to judge. All I hope to do is to place before you my views on the problem.

* * * * * *

The path of social reform, like the path to heaven (at any rate, in India), is strewn with many difficulties. Social reform in India has few friends and many critics. The critics fall into two distinct classes. One class consists of political reformers, and the other of the socialists.

It was at one time recognised that without social efficiency, no permanent progress in the other fields of activity was possible; that owing to mischief wrought by evil customs, Hindu society was not in a state of efficiency; and that ceaseless efforts must be made to eradicate these evils. It was due to the recognition of this fact that the birth of the National Congress was accompanied by the foundation of the Social Conference. While the Congress was concerned with defining the weak points in the political organisation of the country, the Social Conference was engaged in removing the weak points in the social organisation of Hindu society. For some time, the Congress and the Conference worked as two wings of one common activity, and they held their annual sessions in the same pandal.

But soon the two wings developed into two parties, a 'political reform party' and a 'social reform party', between whom there raged a fierce controversy. The 'political reform party' supported the National Congress, and the 'social reform party' supported the Social Conference. The two bodies thus became two hostile camps. The point at issue was whether social reform should precede political reform. For a decade the forces were evenly balanced, and the battle was fought without victory to either side.

It was, however, evident that the fortunes of the Social Conference were ebbing fast. The gentlemen who presided over the sessions of the Social Conference lamented that the majority of the educated Hindus were for political advancement and indifferent to social reform; and that while the number of those who attended the Congress was very large, and the number who did not attend but who sympathised with it was even larger, the number of those who attended the Social Conference was very much smaller.

This indifference—this thinning of its ranks—was soon followed by active hostility from the politicians. Under the leadership of the late Mr Tilak, the courtesy with which the Congress allowed the Social Conference the use of its pandal was withdrawn, and the spirit of enmity went to such a pitch that when the Social Conference desired to erect its own pandal, a threat to burn the pandal was held out by its opponents. Thus, in the course of time the party in favour of political reform won, and the Social Conference vanished and was forgotten.

The speech delivered by Mr W.C. Bonnerjee in 1892 at Allahabad, as president of the eighth session of the Congress, sounds like a funeral oration on the death of the Social Conference, and is so typical of the Congress attitude that I venture to quote from it the following extract. Mr Bonnerjee said:

> I for one have no patience with those who say we shall not be fit for political reform until we reform our social system. I fail to see any connection between the two . . . Are we not fit

> (for political reform) because our widows remain unmarried and our girls are given in marriage earlier than in other countries?... because our wives and daughters do not drive about with us visiting our friends?...because we do not send our daughters to Oxford and Cambridge? (Cheers from the audience)

I have stated the case for political reform as put by Mr Bonnerjee. There were many who were happy that the victory went to the Congress. But those who believe in the importance of social reform may ask, is an argument such as that of Mr Bonnerjee final? Does it prove that the victory went to those who were in the right? Does it prove conclusively that social reform has no bearing on political reform? It will help us to understand the matter if I state the other side of the case. I will draw upon the treatment of the Untouchables for my facts.

Under the rule of the Peshwas in the Maratha country, the Untouchable was not allowed to use the public streets if a Hindu was coming along, lest he should pollute the Hindu by his shadow. The Untouchable was required to have a black thread either on his wrist or around his neck, as a sign or a mark to prevent the Hindus from getting themselves polluted by his touch by mistake. In Poona, the capital of the Peshwa, the Untouchable was required to carry, strung from his waist, a broom to sweep away from behind himself the dust he trod on, lest a Hindu walking on the same dust should be polluted. In Poona, the Untouchable was required to carry an earthen pot hung around his neck wherever he went—for holding his spit, lest his spit falling on the earth should pollute a Hindu who might unknowingly happen to tread on it.

Let me take more recent facts. The tyranny practised by the Hindus upon the Balais, an Untouchable community in Central India, will serve my purpose. You will find a report of this in the *Times of India* of 4th January 1928. The correspondent of the *Times of India* reported that high-caste Hindus—viz., Kalotas, Rajputs and Brahmins, including the Patels and Patwaris of the villages of Kanaria, Bicholi-Hapsi, Bicholi-Mardana, and about fifteen other villages in Indore district (of Indore State)—informed the Balais of their respective villages that if they wished to live among them, they must conform to the following rules:

1. Balais must not wear gold-lace-bordered pugrees.
2. They must not wear dhotis with coloured or fancy borders.
3. They must convey intimation of the death of any Hindu to relatives of the deceased—no matter how far away these relatives may be living.
4. In all Hindu marriages, Balais must play music before the processions and during the marriage.
5. Balai women must not wear gold or silver ornaments; they must not wear fancy gowns or jackets.
6. Balai women must attend all cases of confinement of Hindu women.
7. Balais must render services without demanding remuneration, and must accept whatever a Hindu is pleased to give.
8. If the Balais do not agree to abide by these terms, they must clear out of the villages.

The Balais refused to comply; and the Hindu element proceeded against them. Balais were not allowed to get water from the village wells; they were not allowed to let their cattle graze. Balais were prohibited from passing through land owned by a Hindu, so that if the field of a Balai was surrounded by fields owned by Hindus, the Balai could have no access to his own field. The Hindus also let their cattle graze down the fields of Balais. The Balais submitted petitions to the Darbar against these persecutions; but as they could get no timely relief, and the oppression continued, hundreds of Balais with their wives and children were obliged to abandon their homes—in which their ancestors had lived for generations—and to migrate to adjoining states: that is, to villages in Dhar, Dewas, Bagli, Bhopal, Gwalior and other states.

What happened to them in their new homes may for the present be left out of our consideration.

The incident at Kavitha in Gujarat happened only last year. The Hindus of Kavitha ordered the Untouchables not to insist upon sending their children to the common village school maintained by the government. What sufferings the Untouchables of Kavitha had to undergo, for daring to exercise a civic right against the wishes of the Hindus, is too well known to need detailed description. Another instance occurred in the village of Zanu, in the Ahmedabad district of Gujarat. In November 1935 some Untouchable women of well-to-do families started fetching water in metal pots. The Hindus looked upon the use of metal pots by Untouchables as an affront to their dignity, and assaulted the Untouchable women for their impudence.

A most recent event is reported from the village of Chakwara in Jaipur state. It seems from the reports that have appeared in the newspapers that an Untouchable of Chakwara who had returned from a pilgrimage had arranged to give a dinner to his fellow Untouchables of the village, as an act of religious piety. The host desired to treat the guests to a sumptuous meal, and the items served included ghee (butter) also. But while the assembly of Untouchables was engaged in partaking of the food, the Hindus in their hundreds, armed with lathis, rushed to the scene, despoiled the food, and belaboured the Untouchables who left the food, and ran for their lives. And why was this murderous assault committed on defenceless Untouchables? The reason given is that the Untouchable host was impudent enough to serve ghee, and his Untouchable guests were foolish enough to taste it. Ghee is undoubtedly a luxury for the rich. But no one would think that consumption of ghee was a mark of high social status. The Hindus of Chakwara thought otherwise, and in righteous indignation avenged themselves for the wrong done to them by the Untouchables, who insulted them by treating ghee as an item of their food—which they ought to have known could not be theirs—consistently with the dignity of the Hindus. This means that an Untouchable must not use ghee, even if he can afford to buy it, since it is an act of arrogance towards the Hindus. This happened on or about the 1st of April 1936!

Having stated the facts let me now state the case for social reform. In doing this, I will follow Mr Bonnerjee as nearly as I can, and ask the political minded Hindus, "Are you fit for political power even though you do not allow a large class of your own countrymen like the Untouchables to use public schools? Are you fit for political power even though you do not allow them the use of public wells? Are you fit for political power even though you do not allow them the use of public streets? Are you fit for political power even though you do not allow them to wear what apparel or ornaments they like? Are you fit for political power even though you do not allow them to eat any food they like?" I can ask a string of such questions. But these will suffice.

I wonder what would have been the reply of Mr Bonnerjee. I am sure no sensible man will have the courage to give an affirmative answer. Every Congressman who repeats the dogma of Mill17 that one country is not fit to rule another country, must admit that one class is not fit to rule another class. How is it then that the 'social reform party' lost the battle? To understand this correctly it is necessary to take note of the kind of social reform which the reformers were agitating for. In this connection it is necessary to make a distinction between social reform in the sense of the reform of the Hindu family, and social reform in the sense of the reorganisation and reconstruction of Hindu society. The former has a relation to widow remarriage, child marriage, etc., while the latter relates to the abolition of the caste system.

The Social Conference was a body which mainly concerned itself with the reform of the high-caste Hindu family. It consisted mostly of enlightened high-caste Hindus who did not feel the necessity for agitating for the abolition of caste, or had not the courage to agitate for it. They felt quite naturally a greater urge to remove such evils as enforced widowhood, child marriages, etc.—evils which prevailed among them and which were personally felt by them. They did not stand up for the reform of Hindu society. The battle that was fought centred round the question of the reform of the family. It did not relate to social reform in the sense of the break-up of the caste system. It was never put in issue by the reformers. That is the reason why the 'social reform party' lost.

I am aware that this argument cannot alter the fact that political reform did in fact gain precedence over social reform. But the argument has this much value, if not more: it explains why social reformers lost the battle. It also helps us to understand how limited was the victory which the 'political reform party' obtained over the 'social reform party', and to understand that the view that social reform need not precede political reform is a view which may stand only when by social reform is meant the reform of the family. That political reform cannot with impunity take precedence over social reform in the sense of the reconstruction of society, is a thesis which I am sure cannot be controverted.

That the makers of political constitutions must take account of social forces is a fact which is recognised by no less a person than Ferdinand Lassalle, the friend and co-worker of Karl Marx. In addressing a Prussian audience in 1862, Lassalle said:

> The constitutional questions are in the first instance not questions of right but questions of might. The actual constitution of a country has its existence only in the actual condition of force which exists in the country: hence political constitutions have value and permanence only when they accurately express those conditions of forces which exist in practice within a society.

But it is not necessary to go to Prussia. There is evidence at home. What is the significance of the Communal Award, with its allocation of political power in defined proportions to diverse classes and communities? In my view, its significance lies in this: that political constitution must take note of social organisation. It shows that the politicians who denied that the social problem in India had any bearing on the political problem were forced to reckon with the social problem in devising the constitution. The Communal Award is, so to say, the nemesis following upon the indifference to and neglect of social reform. It is a victory for the 'social reform party', which shows that, though defeated, they were in the right in insisting upon the importance of social reform. Many, I know, will not accept this finding. The view is current—and it is pleasant to believe in it—that the Communal Award is unnatural and that it is the result of an unholy alliance between the minorities and the bureaucracy. I do not wish to rely on the Communal Award as a piece of evidence to support my contention, if it is said that it is not good evidence.

Let us turn to Ireland. What does the history of Irish Home Rule show? It is well known that in the course of the negotiations between the representatives of Ulster and Southern Ireland, Mr Redmond, the representative of Southern Ireland, in order to bring Ulster into a Home Rule constitution common to the whole of Ireland, said to the representatives of Ulster: "Ask any political safeguards you like and you shall have them." What was the reply that Ulstermen gave? Their reply was, "Damn your safeguards, we don't want to be ruled by you on any terms." People who blame the minorities in India ought to consider what would have happened to the political aspirations of the majority, if the minorities had taken the attitude which Ulster took. Judged by the attitude of Ulster to Irish Home Rule, is it nothing that the minorities agreed to be ruled by the majority (which has not shown much sense of statesmanship), provided some safeguards were devised for them? But this is only incidental. The main question is, why did Ulster take this attitude? The only answer I can give is that there was a social problem between Ulster and Southern Ireland: the problem between Catholics and Protestants, which is essentially a problem of caste. That Home Rule in Ireland would be Rome Rule was the way in which the Ulstermen had framed their answer. But that is only another way of stating that it was the social problem of caste between the Catholics and Protestants, which prevented the solution of the political problem. This evidence again is sure to be challenged. It will be urged that here too the hand of the Imperialist was at work.

But my resources are not exhausted. I will give evidence from the history of Rome. Here no one can say that any evil genius was at work. Anyone who has studied the history of Rome will know that the republican constitution of Rome bore marks having strong resemblance to the Communal Award. When the kingship in Rome was abolished, the kingly power or the Imperium was divided between the consuls and the Pontifex Maximus. In the consuls was vested the secular authority of the king, while the latter took over the religious authority of the king. This republican constitution had provided that of the two consuls, one was to be patrician and the other plebeian. The same constitution had also provided that of the priests under the Pontifex Maximus half were to be plebeians and the other half patricians. Why is it that the republican constitution of Rome had these provisions— which, as I said, resemble so strongly the provisions of the Communal Award? The only answer one can get is that the constitution of republican Rome had to take account of the social division between the patricians and the plebeians, who formed two distinct castes.27 To sum up, let political reformers turn in any direction they like, they will find that in the making of a constitution, they cannot ignore the problem arising out of the prevailing social order.

The illustrations which I have taken in support of the proposition that social and religious problems have a bearing on political constitutions seem to be too particular. Perhaps they are. But it should not be supposed that the bearing of the one on the other is limited. On the other hand, one can say that generally speaking, history bears out the proposition that political revolutions have always been preceded by social and religious revolutions. The religious reformation started by Luther was the precursor of the political emancipation of the European people. In England, Puritanism led to the establishment of political liberty. Puritanism founded the new world. It was Puritanism which won the war of American independence, and Puritanism was a religious movement.

The same is true of the Muslim empire. Before the Arabs became a political power, they had undergone a thorough religious revolution started by the Prophet Muhammad. Even Indian history supports the same conclusion. The political revolution led by Chandragupta was preceded by the religious and social revolution of Buddha. The political revolution led by Shivaji was preceded by the religious and social reform brought about by the saints of Maharashtra. The political revolution of the Sikhs was preceded by the religious and social revolution led by Guru Nanak. It is unnecessary to add more illustrations. These will suffice to show that the emancipation of the mind and the soul is a necessary preliminary for the political expansion of the people.

******

Let me now turn to the socialists. Can the socialists ignore the problem arising out of the social order? The socialists of India, following their fellows in Europe, are seeking to apply the economic interpretation of history to the facts of India. They propound that man is an economic creature, that his activities and aspirations are bound by economic facts, that property is the only source of power. They therefore preach that political and social reforms are but gigantic illusions, and that economic reform by equalisation of property must have precedence over every other kind of reform. One may join issue with every one of these premises—on which rests the socialists' case for economic reform as having priority over every other kind of reform. One may contend that the economic motive is not the only motive by which man is actuated. That economic power is the only kind of power, no student of human society can accept.

That the social status of an individual by itself often becomes a source of power and authority is made clear by the sway which the Mahatmas have held over the common man. Why do millionaires in India obey penniless sadhus and fakirs? Why do millions of paupers in India sell their trifling trinkets which constitute their only wealth, and go to Benares and Mecca? That religion is the source of power is illustrated by the history of India, where the priest holds sway over the common man often greater than that of the magistrate, and where everything, even such things as strikes and elections, so easily takes a religious turn and can so easily be given a religious twist.

Take the case of the plebeians of Rome as a further illustration of the power of religion over man. It throws great light on this point. The plebeians had fought for a share in the supreme executive under the Roman Republic, and had secured the appointment of a plebeian consul elected by a separate electorate constituted by the Comitia Centuriata, which was an assembly of plebeians. They wanted a consul of their own because they felt that the patrician consuls used to discriminate against the plebeians in carrying on the administration. They had apparently obtained a great gain, because under the republican constitution of Rome one consul had the power of vetoing an act of the other consul.

But did they in fact gain anything? The answer to this question must be in the negative. The plebeians never could get a plebeian consul who could be said to be a strong man, and who could act independently of the patrician consul. In the ordinary course of things the plebeians should have got a strong plebeian consul, in view of the fact that his election was to be by a separate electorate of plebeians. The question is, why did they fail in getting a strong plebeian to officiate as their consul?

The answer to this question reveals the dominion which religion exercises over the minds of men. It was an accepted creed of the whole Roman populus that no official could enter upon the duties of his office unless the Oracle of Delphi declared that he was acceptable to the goddess. The priests who were in charge of the temple of the goddess of Delphi were all patricians. Whenever therefore the plebeians elected a consul who was known to be a strong party man and opposed to the patricians—or 'communal', to use the term that is current in India—the Oracle invariably declared that he was not acceptable to the goddess. This is how the plebeians were cheated out of their rights.

But what is worthy of note is that the plebeians permitted themselves to be thus cheated because they too, like the patricians, held firmly the belief that the approval of the goddess was a condition precedent to the taking charge by an official of his duties, and that election by the people was not enough. If the plebeians had contended that election was enough and that the approval by the goddess was not necessary, they would have derived the fullest benefit from the political right which they had obtained. But they did not. They agreed to elect another, less suitable to themselves but more suitable to the goddess—which in fact meant more amenable to the patricians. Rather than give up religion, the plebeians gave up the material gain for which they had fought so hard. Does this not show that religion can be a source of power as great as money, if not greater?

The fallacy of the socialists lies in supposing that because in the present stage of European society property as a source of power is predominant, the same is true of India, or the same was true of Europe in the past. Religion, social status, and property are all sources of power and authority which one man has to control the liberty of another. One is predominant at one stage; the other is predominant at another stage. That is the only difference. If liberty is the ideal, and if liberty means the destruction of the dominion which one man holds over another, then obviously it cannot be insisted upon that economic reform must be the one kind of reform worthy of pursuit. If the source of power and dominion is, at any given time or in any given society, social and religious, then social reform and religious reform must be accepted as the necessary sort of reform.

One can thus attack the doctrine of economic interpretation of history adopted by the socialists of India. But I recognise that the economic interpretation of history is not necessary for the validity of the socialist contention that equalisation of property is the only real reform and that it must precede everything else. However, what I would like to ask the socialists is this: Can you have economic reform without first bringing about a reform of the social order? The socialists of India do not seem to have considered this question. I do not wish to do them an injustice. I give below a quotation from a letter which a prominent socialist wrote a few days ago to a friend of mine, in which he said, "I do not believe that we can build up a free society in India so long as there is a trace of this ill-treatment and suppression of one class by another. Believing as I do in a socialist ideal, inevitably I believe in perfect equality in the treatment of various classes and groups. I think that socialism offers the only true remedy for this as well as other problems."

Now the question that I would like to ask is: Is it enough for a socialist to say, 'I believe in perfect equality in the treatment of the various classes?" To say that such a belief is enough is to disclose a complete lack of understanding of what is involved in socialism. If socialism is a practical programme and is not merely an ideal, distant and far off, the question for a socialist is not whether he believes in equality. The question for him is whether he minds one class ill-treating and suppressing another class as a matter of system, as a matter of principle—and thus allow tyranny and oppression to continue to divide one class from another.

Let me analyse the factors that are involved in the realisation of socialism, in order to explain fully my point. Now it is obvious that the economic reform contemplated by the socialists cannot come about unless there is a revolution resulting in the seizure of power. That seizure of power must be by a proletariat. The first question I ask is: Will the proletariat of India combine to bring about this revolution? What will move men to such an action? It seems to me that, other things being equal, the only thing that will move one man to take such an action is the feeling that other men with whom he is acting are actuated by feelings of equality and fraternity and—above all—of justice. Men will not join in a revolution for the equalisation of property unless they know that after the revolution is achieved they will be treated equally, and that there will be no discrimination of caste and creed.

The assurance of a socialist leading the revolution that he does not believe in caste, I am sure, will not suffice. The assurance must be the assurance proceeding from a much deeper foundation—namely, the mental attitude of the compatriots towards one another in their spirit of personal equality and fraternity. Can it be said that the proletariat of India, poor as it is, recognises no distinctions except that of the rich and the poor? Can it be said that the poor in India recognise no such distinctions of caste or creed, high or low? If the fact is that they do, what unity of front can be expected from such a proletariat in its action against the rich? How can there be a revolution if the proletariat cannot present a united front?

Suppose for the sake of argument that by some freak of fortune a revolution does take place and the socialists come into power, will they not have to deal with the problems created by the particular social order prevalent in India? I can't see how a socialist state in India can function for a second without having to grapple with the problems created by the prejudices which make Indian people observe the distinctions of high and low, clean and unclean. If socialists are not to be content with the mouthing of fine phrases, if the socialists wish to make socialism a definite reality, then they must recognise that the problem of social reform is fundamental, and that for them there is no escape from it.

That the social order prevalent in India is a matter which a socialist must deal with; that unless he does so he cannot achieve his revolution; and that if he does achieve it as a result of good fortune, he will have to grapple with the social order if he wishes to realise his ideal—is a proposition which in my opinion is incontrovertible. He will be compelled to take account of caste after the revolution, if he does not take account of it before the revolution. This is only another way of saying that, turn in any direction you like, caste is the monster that crosses your path. You cannot have political reform, you cannot have economic reform, unless you kill this monster.

* * * * * *

It is a pity that caste even today has its defenders. The defences are many. It is defended on the ground that the caste system is but another name for division of labour; and if division of labour is a necessary feature of every civilised society, then it is argued that there is nothing wrong in the caste system. Now the first thing that is to be urged against this view is that the caste system is not merely a division of labour. *It is also a division of labourers.* Civilised society undoubtedly needs division of labour. But in no civilised society is division of labour accompanied by this unnatural division of labourers into watertight compartments. The caste system is not merely a division of labourers—which is quite different from division of labour—it is a hierarchy in which the divisions of labourers are graded one above the other. In no other country is the division of labour accompanied by this gradation of labourers.

There is also a third point of criticism against this view of the caste system. This division of labour is not spontaneous; it is not based on natural aptitudes. Social and individual efficiency requires us to develop the capacity of an individual to the point of competency to choose and to make his own career. This principle is violated in the caste system, in so far as it involves an attempt to appoint tasks to individuals in advance—selected not on the basis of trained original capacities, but on that of the social status of the parents.

Looked at from another point of view, this stratification of occupations which is the result of the caste system is positively pernicious. Industry is never static. It undergoes rapid and abrupt changes. With such changes, an individual must be free to change his occupation. Without such freedom to adjust himself to changing circumstances, it would be impossible for him to gain his livelihood. Now the caste system will not allow Hindus to take to occupations where they are wanted, if they do not belong to them by heredity. If a Hindu is seen to starve rather than take to new occupations not assigned to his caste, the reason is to be found in the caste system. By not permitting readjustment of occupations, caste becomes a direct cause of much of the unemployment we see in the country.

As a form of division of labour, the caste system suffers from another serious defect. The division of labour brought about by the caste system is not a division based on choice. Individual sentiment, individual preference, has no place in it. It is based on the dogma of predestination. Considerations of social efficiency would compel us to recognise that the greatest evil in the industrial system is not so much poverty and the suffering that it involves, as the fact that so many persons have callings which make no appeal to those who are engaged in them. Such callings constantly provoke one to aversion, ill will and the desire to evade.

There are many occupations in India which, on account of the fact that they are regarded as degraded by the Hindus, provoke those who are engaged in them to aversion. There is a constant desire to evade and escape from such occupations, which arises solely because of the blighting effect which they produce upon those who follow them, owing to the slight and stigma cast upon them by the Hindu religion. What efficiency can there be in a system under which neither men's hearts nor their minds are in their work? As an economic organisation caste is therefore a harmful institution, inasmuch as it involves the subordination of man's natural powers and inclinations to the exigencies of social rules.

* * * * * *

Some have dug a biological trench in defence of the caste system. It is said that the object of caste was to preserve purity of race and purity of blood. Now ethnologists are of the opinion that men of pure race exist nowhere and that there has been a mixture of all races in all parts of the world. Especially is this the case with the people of India. Mr D.R. Bhandarkar in his paper on "Foreign Elements in the Hindu Population" has stated that "There is hardly a class or caste in India which has not a foreign strain in it. There is an admixture of alien blood not only among the warrior classes—the Rajputs and the Marathas— but also among the Brahmins who are under the happy delusion that they are free from all foreign elements." The caste system cannot be said to have grown as a means of preventing the admixture of races, or as a means of maintaining purity of blood.

As a matter of fact the caste system came into being long after the different races of India had commingled in blood and culture. To hold that distinctions of castes are really distinctions of race, and to treat different castes as though they were so many different races, is a gross perversion of facts. What racial affinity is there between the Brahmin of the Punjab and the Brahmin of Madras? What racial affinity is there between the Untouchable of Bengal and the Untouchable of Madras? What racial difference is there between the Brahmin of the Punjab and the Chamar of the Punjab? What racial difference is there between the Brahmin of Madras and the Pariah of Madras? The Brahmin of the Punjab is racially of the same stock as the Chamar of the Punjab, and the Brahmin of Madras is of the same race as the Pariah of Madras.

The caste system does not demarcate racial division. The caste system is a social division of people of the same race. Assuming it, however, to be a case of racial divisions, one may ask: What harm could there be if a mixture of races and of blood was permitted to take place in India by intermarriage between different castes? Men are no doubt divided from animals by so deep a distinction that science recognises men and animals as two distinct species.* But even scientists who believe in purity of races do not assert that the different races constitute different species of men. They are only varieties of one and the same species. As such they can interbreed and produce an offspring which is capable of breeding and which is not sterile.

An immense lot of nonsense is talked about heredity and eugenics in defence of the caste system. Few would object to the caste system if it was in accord with the basic principle of eugenics, because few can object to the improvement of the race by judicious mating. But one fails to understand how the caste system secures judicious mating. The caste system is a negative thing. It merely prohibits persons belonging to different castes from intermarrying. It is not a positive method of selecting which two among a given caste should marry.

If caste is eugenic in origin, then the origin of sub-castes must also be eugenic. But can anyone seriously maintain that the origin of sub-castes is eugenic? I think it would be absurd to contend for such a proposition, and for a very obvious reason. If caste means race, then differences of sub-castes cannot mean differences of race, because sub-castes become *ex hypothesi* sub-divisions of one and the same race. Consequently the bar against inter-marrying and inter-dining between sub-castes cannot be for the purpose of maintaining purity of race or of blood. If sub-castes cannot be eugenic in origin, there cannot be any substance in the contention that caste is eugenic in origin.

Again, if caste is eugenic in origin one can understand the bar against intermarriage. But what is the purpose of the interdict placed on inter-dining between castes and sub-castes alike? Inter-dining cannot infect blood, and therefore cannot be the cause either of the improvement or of the deterioration of the race.

This shows that caste has no scientific origin, and that those who are attempting to give it a eugenic basis are trying to support by science what is grossly unscientific. Even today, eugenics cannot become a practical possibility unless we have definite knowledge regarding the laws of heredity. Prof Bateson in his *Mendel's Principles of Heredity* says, "There is nothing in the descent of the higher mental qualities to suggest that they follow any single system of transmission. It is likely that both they and the more marked developments of physical powers result rather from the coincidence of numerous factors than from the possession of any one genetic element." To argue that the caste system was eugenic in its conception is to attribute to the forefathers of present-day Hindus a knowledge of heredity which even the modern scientists do not possess.

A tree should be judged by the fruits it yields. If caste is eugenic, what sort of a race of men should it have produced? Physically speaking the Hindus are a C3 people. They are a race of pygmies and dwarfs, stunted in stature and wanting in stamina. It is a nation nine-tenths of which is declared to be unfit for military service. This shows that the caste system does not embody the eugenics of modern scientists. It is a social system which embodies the arrogance and selfishness of a perverse section of the Hindus who were superior enough in social status to set it in fashion, and who had the authority to force it on their inferiors.

* * * * * *

Caste does not result in economic efficiency. Caste cannot improve, and has not improved, race. Caste has, however, done one thing. It has completely disorganised and demoralised the Hindus.

The first and foremost thing that must be recognised is that Hindu society is a myth. The name Hindu is itself a foreign name. It was given by the Mahomedans to the natives for the purpose of distinguishing themselves. It does not occur in any Sanskrit work prior to the Mahomedan invasion. They did not feel the necessity of a common name, because they had no conception of their having constituted a community. Hindu society as such does not exist. It is only a collection of castes. Each caste is conscious of its existence. Its survival is the be all and end-all of its existence. Castes do not even form a federation. A caste has no feeling that it is affiliated to other castes, except when there is a Hindu-Moslem riot. On all other occasions each caste endeavours to segregate itself and to distinguish itself from other castes.

Each caste not only dines among itself and marries among itself, but each caste prescribes its own distinctive dress. What other explanation can there be of the innumerable styles of dress worn by the men and women of India, which so amuse the tourists? Indeed, the ideal Hindu must be like a rat living in his own hole, refusing to have any contact with others. There is an utter lack among the Hindus of what the sociologists call 'consciousness of kind'. There is no Hindu consciousness of kind. In every Hindu the consciousness that exists is the consciousness of his caste. That is the reason why the Hindus cannot be said to form a society or a nation.

There are, however, many Indians whose patriotism does not permit them to admit that Indians are not a nation, that they are only an amorphous mass of people. They have insisted that underlying the apparent diversity there is a fundamental unity which marks the life of the Hindus, inasmuch as there is a similarity of those habits and customs, beliefs and thoughts, which obtain all over the continent of India. Similarity in habits and customs, beliefs and thoughts, there is. But one cannot accept the conclusion that therefore, the Hindus constitute a society. To do so is to misunderstand the essentials which go to make up a society. Men do not become a society by living in physical proximity, any more than a man ceases to be a member of his society by living so many miles away from other men.

Secondly, similarity in habits and customs, beliefs and thoughts, is not enough to constitute men into society. Things may be passed physically from one to another like bricks. In the same way habits and customs, beliefs and thoughts of one group may be taken over by another group, and there may thus appear a similarity between the two. Culture spreads by diffusion, and that is why one finds similarity between various primitive tribes in the matter of their habits and customs, beliefs and thoughts, although they do not live in proximity. But no one could say that because there was this similarity, the primitive tribes constituted one society. This is because similarity in certain things is not enough to constitute a society.

Men constitute a society because they have things which they possess in common. To have similar things is totally different from possessing things in common. And the only way by which men can come to possess things in common with one another is by being in communication with one another. This is merely another way of saying that society continues to exist by communication—indeed, in communication. To make it concrete, it is not enough if men act in a way which agrees with the acts of others. Parallel activity, even if similar, is not sufficient to bind men into a society.

This is proved by the fact that the festivals observed by the different castes amongst the Hindus are the same. Yet these parallel performances of similar festivals by the different castes have not bound them into one integral whole. For that purpose what is necessary is for a man to share and participate in a common activity, so that the same emotions are aroused in him that animate the others. Making the individual a sharer or partner in the associated activity, so that he feels its success as his success, its failure as his failure, is the real thing that binds men and makes a society of them. The caste system prevents common activity; and by preventing common activity, it has prevented the Hindus from becoming a society with a unified life and a consciousness of its own being.

* * * * * *

The Hindus often complain of the isolation and exclusiveness of a gang or a clique and blame them for anti-social spirit. But they conveniently forget that this anti-social spirit is the worst feature of their own caste system. One caste enjoys singing a hymn of hate against another caste as much as the Germans enjoyed singing their hymn of hate against the English during the last war. The literature of the Hindus is full of caste genealogies in which an attempt is made to give a noble origin to one caste and an ignoble origin to other castes. The Sahyadrikhand is a notorious instance of this class of literature.

This anti-social spirit is not confined to caste alone. It has gone deeper and has poisoned the mutual relations of the sub-castes as well. In my province the Golak Brahmins, Deorukha Brahmins, Karada Brahmins, Palshe Brahmins, and Chitpavan Brahmins all claim to be sub-divisions of the Brahmin caste. But the anti-social spirit that prevails between them is quite as marked and quite as virulent as the anti-social spirit that prevails between them and other non-Brahmin castes. There is nothing strange in this. An anti-social spirit is found wherever one group has 'interests of its own' which shut it out from full interaction with other groups, so that its prevailing purpose is protection of what it has got.

This anti-social spirit, this spirit of protecting their own interests, is as much a marked feature of the different castes in their isolation from one another as it is of nations in their isolation. The Brahmin's primary concern is to protect 'his interests' against those of the non-Brahmins; and the non-Brahmins' primary concern is to protect their interests against those of the Brahmins. The Hindus, therefore, are not merely an assortment of castes, but are so many warring groups, each living for itself and for its selfish ideal.

There is another feature of caste which is deplorable. The ancestors of the present-day English fought on one side or the other in the Wars of the Roses and the Cromwellian War. But the descendants of those who fought on the one side do not bear any animosity—any grudge—against the descendants of those who fought on the other side. The feud is forgotten. But the present day non-Brahmins cannot forgive the present-day Brahmins for the insult their ancestors gave to Shivaji. The present-day Kayasthas will not forgive the present-day Brahmins for the infamy cast upon their forefathers by the forefathers of the latter. To what is this difference due? Obviously to the caste system. The existence of caste and caste consciousness has served to keep the memory of past feuds between castes green, and has prevented solidarity.

* * * * * *

The recent discussion about the excluded and partially excluded areas has served to draw attention to the position of what are called the aboriginal tribes in India. They number about thirteen million, if not more. Apart from the question of whether their exclusion from the new constitution is proper or improper, the fact still remains that these aborigines have remained in their primitive uncivilised state in a land which boasts of a civilisation thousands of years old. Not only are they not civilised, but some of them follow pursuits which have led to their being classified as criminals.

Thirteen million people living in the midst of civilisation are still in a savage state, and are leading the life of hereditary criminals! But the Hindus have never felt ashamed of it. This is a phenomenon which in my view is quite unparalleled. What is the cause of this shameful state of affairs? Why has no attempt been made to civilise these aborigines and to lead them to take to a more honourable way of making a living?

The Hindus will probably seek to account for this savage state of the aborigines by attributing to them congenital stupidity. They will probably not admit that the aborigines have remained savages because they had made no effort to civilise them, to give them medical aid, to reform them, to make them good citizens. But supposing a Hindu wished to do what the Christian missionary is doing for these aborigines, could he have done it? I submit not. Civilising the aborigines means adopting them as your own, living in their midst, and cultivating fellow-feeling—in short, loving them. How is it possible for a Hindu to do this? His whole life is one anxious effort to preserve his caste. Caste is his precious possession which he must save at any cost. He cannot consent to lose it by establishing contact with the aborigines, the remnants of the hateful *anayas* of the Vedic days.

Not that a Hindu could not be taught the sense of duty to fallen humanity, but the trouble is that no amount of sense of duty can enable him to overcome his duty to preserve his caste. Caste is, therefore, the real explanation as to why the Hindu has let the savage remain a savage in the midst of his civilisation without blushing, or without feeling any sense of remorse or repentance. The Hindu has not realised that these aborigines are a source of potential danger. If these savages remain savages, they may not do any harm to the Hindus. But if they are reclaimed by non-Hindus and converted to their faiths, they will swell the ranks of the enemies of the Hindus. If this happens, the Hindu will have to thank himself and his caste system.

* * * * * *

Not only has the Hindu made no effort for the humanitarian cause of civilising the savages, but the higher-caste Hindus have deliberately prevented the lower castes who are within the pale of Hinduism from rising to the cultural level of the higher castes. I will give two instances, one of the Sonars and the other of the Pathare Prabhus. Both are communities quite well known in Maharashtra. Like the rest of the communities desiring to raise their status, these two communities were at one time endeavouring to adopt some of the ways and habits of the Brahmins.

The Sonars were styling themselves Daivadnya Brahmins and were wearing their dhotis with folds in them, and using the word 'namaskar' for salutation. Both the folded way of wearing the dhoti and the namaskar were special to the Brahmins. The Brahmins did not like this imitation and this attempt by Sonars to pass off as Brahmins. Under the authority of the Peshwas, the Brahmins successfully put down this attempt on the part of the Sonars to adopt the ways of the Brahmins. They even got the president of the councils of the East India Company's settlement in Bombay to issue a prohibitory order against the Sonars residing in Bombay.

At one time the Pathare Prabhus had widow remarriage as a custom of their caste. This custom of widow remarriage was later on looked upon as a mark of social inferiority by some members of the caste, especially because it was contrary to the custom prevalent among the Brahmins. With the object of raising the status of their community, some Pathare Prabhus sought to stop this practice of widow remarriage that was prevalent in their caste. The community was divided into two camps, one for and the other against the innovation. The Peshwas took the side of those in favour of widow remarriage, and thus virtually prohibited the Pathare Prabhus from following the ways of the Brahmins.

The Hindus criticise the Mahomedans for having spread their religion by the use of the sword. They also ridicule Christianity on the score of the Inquisition. But really speaking, who is better and more worthy of our respect—the Mahomedans and Christians who attempted to thrust down the throats of unwilling persons what they regarded as necessary for their salvation, or the Hindu who would not spread the light, who would endeavour to keep others in darkness, who would not consent to share his intellectual and social inheritance with those who are ready and willing to make it a part of their own makeup? I have no hesitation in saying that if the Mahomedan has been cruel, the Hindu has been mean; and meanness is worse than cruelty.

* * * * * *

Whether the Hindu religion was or was not a missionary religion has been a controversial issue. Some hold the view that it was never a missionary religion. Others hold that it was. That the Hindu religion was once a missionary religion must be admitted. It could not have spread over the face of India, if it was not a missionary religion. That today it is not a missionary religion is also a fact which must be accepted. The question therefore is not whether or not the Hindu religion was a missionary religion. The real question is, why did the Hindu religion cease to be a missionary religion?

My answer is this: the Hindu religion ceased to be a missionary religion when the caste system grew up among the

Hindus. Caste is inconsistent with conversion. Inculcation of beliefs and dogmas is not the only problem that is involved in conversion. To find a place for the convert in the social life of the community is another, and a much more important, problem that arises in connection with conversion. That problem is where to place the convert, in what caste? It is a problem which must baffle every Hindu wishing to make aliens convert to his religion.

Unlike a club, the membership of a caste is not open to all and sundry.72 The law of caste confines its membership to persons born in the caste. Castes are autonomous, and there is no authority anywhere to compel a caste to admit a newcomer to its social life. Hindu society being a collection of castes, and each caste being a closed corporation, there is no place for a convert. Thus, it is caste which has prevented the Hindus from expanding and from absorbing other religious communities. So long as caste remains, Hindu religion cannot be made a missionary religion, and *shuddhi* will be both a folly and a futility.

* * * * * *

The reasons which have made *shuddhi* impossible for Hindus are also responsible for making *sangathan* impossible. The idea underlying *sangathan* is to remove from the mind of the Hindu that timidity and cowardice which so painfully mark him off from the Mahomedan and the Sikh, and which have led him to adopt the low ways of treachery and cunning for protecting himself. The question naturally arises: From where does the Sikh or the Mahomedan derive his strength, which makes him brave and fearless? I am sure it is not due to relative superiority of physical strength, diet or drill. It is due to the strength arising out of the feeling that all Sikhs will come to the rescue of a Sikh when he is in danger, and that all Mahomedans will rush to save a Muslim if he is attacked.

The Hindu can derive no such strength. He cannot feel assured that his fellows will come to his help. Being one and fated to be alone, he remains powerless, develops timidity and cowardice, and in a fight surrenders or runs away. The Sikh as well as the Muslim stands fearless and gives battle, because he knows that though one, he will not be alone. The presence of this belief in the one helps him to hold out, and the absence of it in the other makes him to give way.

If you pursue this matter further and ask what is it that enables the Sikh and the Mahomedan to feel so assured, and why is the Hindu filled with such despair in the matter of help and assistance, you will find that the reasons for this difference lie in the difference in their associated mode of living. The associated mode of life practised by the Sikhs and the Mahomedans produces fellow-feeling. The associated mode of life of the Hindus does not. Among Sikhs and Muslims there is a social cement which makes them *bhais*. Among Hindus there is no such cement, and one Hindu does not regard another Hindu as his bhai. This explains why a Sikh says and feels that one Sikh, or one Khalsa, is equal to *sava lakh* men. This explains why one Mahomedan is equal to a crowd of Hindus. This difference is undoubtedly a difference due to caste. So long as caste remains, there will be no sangathan; and so long as there is no sangathan the Hindu will remain weak and meek.

The Hindus claim to be a very tolerant people. In my opinion this is mistake. On many occasions they can be intolerant, and if on some occasions they are tolerant, that is because they are too weak to oppose or too indifferent to oppose. This indifference of the Hindus has become so much a part of their nature that a Hindu will quite meekly tolerate an insult as well as a wrong. You see amongst them, to use the words of Morris, "The great treading down the little, the strong beating down the weak, cruel men fearing not, kind men daring not and wise men caring not." With the Hindu gods all-forbearing, it is not difficult to imagine the pitiable condition of the wronged and the oppressed among the Hindus. Indifferentism is the worst kind of disease that can infect a people. Why is the Hindu so indifferent? In my opinion this indifferentism is the result of the caste system, which has made sangathan and cooperation even for a good cause impossible.

The assertion by the individual of his own opinions and beliefs, his own independence and interest—over and against group standards, group authority, and group interests—is the beginning of all reform. But whether the reform will continue depends upon what scope the group affords for such individual assertion. If the group is tolerant and fair-minded in dealing with such individuals, they will continue to assert, and in the end will succeed in converting their fellows. On the other hand if the group is intolerant, and does not bother about the means it adopts to stifle such individuals, they will perish and the reform will die out.

Now a caste has an unquestioned right to excommunicate any man who is guilty of breaking the rules of the caste; and when it is realised that excommunication involves a complete cesser of social intercourse, it will be agreed that as a form of punishment there is really little to choose between excommunication and death. No wonder individual Hindus have not had the courage to assert their independence by breaking the barriers of cast.

It is true that man cannot get on with his fellows. But it is also true that he cannot do without them. He would like to have the society of his fellows on his terms. If he cannot get it on his terms, then he will be ready to have it on any terms, even amounting to complete surrender. This is because he cannot do without society. A caste is ever ready to take advantage of the helplessness of a man, and to insist upon complete conformity to its code in letter and in spirit.

A caste can easily organise itself into a conspiracy to make the life of a reformer hell; and if a conspiracy is a crime, I do not understand why such a nefarious act as an attempt to excommunicate a person for daring to act contrary to the rules of caste should not be made an offence punishable by law. But as it is, even law gives each caste autonomy to regulate its membership and punish dissenters with excommunication. Caste in the hands of the orthodox has been a powerful weapon for persecuting the reformers and for killing all reform.

* * * * * *

The effect of caste on the ethics of the Hindus is simply deplorable. Caste has killed public spirit. Caste has destroyed the sense of public charity. Caste has made public opinion impossible. A Hindu's public is his caste. His responsibility is only to his caste. His loyalty is restricted only to his caste. Virtue has become caste-ridden, and morality has become caste-bound. There is no sympathy for the deserving. There is no appreciation of the meritorious. There is no charity to the needy. Suffering as such calls for no response. There is charity, but it begins with caste and ends with caste. There is sympathy, but not for men of other castes.

Would a Hindu acknowledge and follow the leadership of a great and good man? The case of a Mahatma apart, the answer must be that he will follow a leader if he is a man of his caste. A Brahmin will follow a leader only if he is a Brahmin, a Kayastha if he is a Kayastha, and so on. The capacity to appreciate merits in a man, apart from his caste, does not exist in a Hindu. There is appreciation of virtue, but only when the man is a fellow caste-man. The whole morality is as bad as tribal morality. My caste-man, right or wrong; my caste-man, good or bad. It is not a case of standing by virtue or not standing by vice. It is a case of standing by, or not standing by, caste. Have not Hindus committed treason against their country in the interests of their castes?

* * * * * *

I would not be surprised if some of you have grown weary listening to this tiresome tale of the sad effects which caste has produced. There is nothing new in it. I will therefore turn to the constructive side of the problem. What is your ideal society if you do not want caste, is a question that is bound to be asked of you. If you ask me, my ideal would be a society based on liberty, equality, and fraternity. And why not?

What objection can there be to fraternity? I cannot imagine any. An ideal society should be mobile, should be full of channels for conveying a change taking place in one part to other parts. In an ideal society there should be many interests consciously communicated and shared. There should be varied and free points of contact with other modes of association. In other words there must be social endosmosis. This is fraternity, which is only another name for democracy. Democracy is not merely a form of government. It is primarily a mode of associated living, of conjoint communicated experience. It is essentially an attitude of respect and reverence towards fellow men.

Any objection to liberty? Few object to liberty in the sense of a right to free movement, in the sense of a right to life and limb. There is no objection to liberty in the sense of a right to property, tools and materials, as being necessary for earning a living, to keep the body in a due state of health. Why not allow a person the liberty to benefit from an effective and competent use of a person's powers? The supporters of caste who would allow liberty in the sense of a right to life, limb, and property, would not readily consent to liberty in this sense, inasmuch as it involves liberty to choose one's profession.

But to object to this kind of liberty is to perpetuate slavery. For slavery does not merely mean a legalised form of subjection. It means a state of society in which some men are forced to accept from others the purposes which control their conduct. This condition obtains even where there is no slavery in the legal sense. It is found where, as in the caste system, some persons are compelled to carry on certain prescribed callings which are not of their choice.

Any objection to equality? This has obviously been the most contentious part of the slogan of the French Revolution. The objections to equality may be sound, and one may have to admit that all men are not equal. But what of that? Equality may be a fiction, but nonetheless one must accept it as the governing principle. A man's power is dependent upon (1) physical heredity; (2) social inheritance or endowment in the form of parental care, education, accumulation of scientific knowledge, everything which enables him to be more efficient than the savage; and finally, (3) on his own efforts. In all these three respects men are undoubtedly unequal. But the question is, shall we treat them as unequal because they are unequal? This is a question which the opponents of equality must answer.

From the standpoint of the individualist, it may be just to treat men unequally so far as their efforts are unequal. It may be desirable to give as much incentive as possible to the full development of everyone's powers. But what would happen if men were treated as unequally as they are unequal in the first two respects? It is obvious that those individuals also in whose favour there is birth, education, family name, business connections, and inherited wealth, would be selected in the race. But selection under such circumstances would not be a selection of the able. It would be the selection of the privileged. The reason, therefore, which forces that in the third respect we should treat men unequally, demands that in the first two respects we should treat men as equally as possible.

On the other hand, it can be urged that if it is good for the social body to get the most out of its members, it can get the most out of them only by making them equal as far as possible at the very start of the race. That is one reason why we cannot escape equality. But there is another reason why we must accept equality. A statesman is concerned with vast numbers of people. He has neither the time nor the knowledge to draw fine distinctions and to treat each one equitably, i.e., according to need or according to capacity. However desirable or reasonable an equitable treatment of men may be, humanity is not capable of assortment and classification. The statesman, therefore, must follow some rough and ready rule, and that rough and ready rule is to treat all men alike, not because they are alike but because classification and assortment is impossible. The doctrine of equality is glaringly fallacious but, taking all in all, it is the only way a statesman can proceed in politics—which is a severely practical affair and which demands a severely practical test.

* * * * * *

But there is a set of reformers who hold out a different ideal. They go by the name of the Arya Samajists, and their ideal of social organisation is what is called *chaturvarnya,* or the division of society into four classes instead of the four thousand castes that we have in India. To make it more attractive and to disarm opposition, the protagonists of chaturvarnya take great care to point out that their chaturvarnya is based not on birth but on *guna* (worth). At the outset, I must confess that notwithstanding the worth-basis of this chaturvarnya, it is an ideal to which I cannot reconcile myself.

In the first place, if under the chaturvarnya of the Arya Samajists an individual is to take his place in Hindu society according to his worth, I do not understand why the Arya Samajists insist upon labelling men as Brahmin, Ḳshatriya, Vaishya and Shudra. A learned man would be honoured without his being labelled a Brahmin. A soldier would be respected without his being designated a Kshatriya. If European society honours its soldiers and its servants without giving them permanent labels, why should Hindu society find it difficult to do so, is a question which Arya Samajists have not cared to consider.

There is another objection to the continuance of these labels. All reform consists in a change in the notions, sentiments and mental attitudes of the people towards men and things. It is common experience that certain names become associated with certain notions and sentiments which determine a person's attitude towards men and things. The names Brahmin, Kshatriya, Vaishya and Shudra are names which are associated with a definite and fixed notion in the mind of every Hindu. That notion is that of a hierarchy based on birth.

So long as these names continue, Hindus will continue to think of the Brahmin, Kshatriya, Vaishya and Shudra as hierarchical divisions of high and low, based on birth, and to act accordingly. The Hindu must be made to unlearn all this. But how can this happen if the old labels remain and continue to recall to his mind old notions? If new notions are to be inculcated in the minds of people, it is necessary to give them new names. To continue the old names is to make the reform futile. To allow this chaturvarnya based on worth to be designated by such stinking labels as Brahmin, Kshatriya, Vaishya, Shudra, indicative of social divisions based on birth, is a snare.

* * * * * *

To me this chaturvarnya with its old labels is utterly repellent, and my whole being rebels against it. But I do not wish to rest my objection to chaturvarnya on mere grounds of sentiments. There are more solid grounds on which I rely for my opposition to it. A close examination of this ideal has convinced me that as a system of social organisation, chaturvarnya is impracticable, is harmful, and has turned out to be a miserable failure. From a practical point of view, the system of chaturvarnya raises several difficulties which its protagonists do not seem to have taken into account. The principle underlying caste is fundamentally different from the principle underlying chaturvarnya. Not only are they fundamentally different, but they are also fundamentally opposed.

The former, chaturvarnya, is based on worth. How are you going to compel people who have acquired a higher status based on birth, without reference to their worth, to vacate that status? How are you going to compel people to recognise the status due to a man, in accordance with his worth, who is occupying a lower status based on his birth? For this, you must first break up the caste system, in order to be able to establish the chaturvarnya system. How are you going to reduce the four thousand castes, based on birth, to the four varnas, based on worth? This is the first difficulty which the protagonists of chaturvarnya must grapple with.

There is a second difficulty which the protagonists of chaturvarnya must grapple with, if they wish to make the establishment of chaturvarnya a success. Chaturvarnya presupposes that you can classify people into four definite classes. Is this possible? In this respect, the ideal of chaturvarnya has, as you will see, a close affinity to the Platonic ideal. To Plato, men fell by nature into three classes. In some individuals, he believed, mere appetites dominated. He assigned them to the labouring and trading classes. Others revealed to him that over and above appetites, they had a courageous disposition. He classed them as defenders in war and guardians of internal peace. Others showed a capacity to grasp the universal—the reason underlying things. He made them the law-givers of the people.

The criticism to which Plato's *Republic* is subject is also the criticism which must apply to the system of chaturvarnya, in so far as it proceeds upon the possibility of an accurate classification of men into four distinct classes. The chief criticism against Plato is that his idea of lumping individuals into a few sharply marked-off classes is a very superficial view of man and his powers. Plato had no perception of the uniqueness of every individual, of his incommensurability with others, of each individual as forming a class of his own. He had no recognition of the infinite diversity of active tendencies, and the combination of tendencies of which an individual is capable. To him, there were types of faculties or powers in the individual constitution.

All this is demonstrably wrong. Modern science has shown that the lumping together of individuals into a few sharply marked-off classes is a superficial view of man, not worthy of serious consideration. Consequently, the utilisation of the qualities of individuals is incompatible with their stratification by classes, since the qualities of individuals are so variable. Chaturvarnya must fail for the very reason for which Plato's Republic must fail—namely, that it is not possible to pigeon men into holes according to class. That it is impossible to accurately classify people into four definite classes is proved by the fact that the original four classes have now become four thousand castes.

There is a third difficulty in the way of the establishment of the system of chaturvarnya. How are you going to maintain the system of chaturvarnya, supposing it was established? One important requirement for the successful working of chaturvarnya is the maintenance of the penal system which could maintain it by its sanction. The system of chaturvarnya must perpetually face the problem of the transgressor. Unless there is a penalty attached to the act of transgression, men will not keep to their respective classes. The whole system will break down, being contrary to human nature. Chaturvarnya cannot subsist by its own inherent goodness. It must be enforced by law.

That without penal sanction the ideal of chaturvarnya cannot be realised is proved by the story in the Ramayana of Rama killing Shambuka. Some people seem to blame Rama because he wantonly and without reason killed Shambuka. But to blame Rama for killing Shambuka is to misunderstand the whole situation. Ram Raj was a raj based on chaturvarnya. As a king, Rama was bound to maintain chaturvarnya. It was his duty therefore to kill Shambuka, the Shudra who had transgressed his class and wanted to be a Brahmin. This is the reason why Rama killed Shambuka. But this also shows that penal sanction is necessary for the maintenance of chaturvarnya. Not only penal sanction is necessary, but the penalty of death is necessary. That is why Rama did not inflict on Shambuka a lesser punishment. That is why the *Manusmriti* prescribes such heavy sentences as cutting off the tongue, or pouring of molten lead in the ears, of the Shudra who recites or hears the Veda. The supporters of chaturvarnya must give an assurance that they could successfully classify men, and that they could induce modern society in the twentieth century to re-forge the penal sanctions of the *Manusmriti*.

The protagonists of chaturvarnya do not seem to have considered what is to happen to women in their system. Are they also to be divided into four classes, Brahmin, Kshatriya, Vaishya and Shudra? Or are they to be allowed to take the status of their husbands? If the status of the woman is to be the consequence of marriage, what becomes of the underlying principle of chaturvarnya—namely, that the status of a person should be based upon the worth of that person? If they are to be classified according to their worth, is their classification to be nominal or real?

If it is to be nominal, then it is useless; and then the protagonists of chaturvarnya must admit that their system does not apply to women. If it is real, are the protagonists of chaturvarnya prepared to follow the logical consequences of applying it to women? They must be prepared to have women priests and women soldiers. Hindu society has grown accustomed to women teachers and women barristers. It may grow accustomed to women brewers and women butchers. But he would be a bold person who would say that it will allow women priests and women soldiers. But that will be the logical outcome of applying chaturvarnya to women. Given these difficulties, I think no one except a congenital idiot could hope for and believe in a successful regeneration of chaturvarnya.

******

Assuming that chaturvarnya is practicable, I contend that it is the most vicious system. That the Brahmins should cultivate knowledge, that the Kshatriya should bear arms, that the Vaishya should trade, and that the Shudra should serve, sounds as though it was a system of division of labour. Whether the theory was intended to state that the Shudra need not, or whether it was intended to lay down that he must not, is an interesting question. The defenders of chaturvarnya give it the first meaning. They say, why need the Shudra trouble to acquire wealth, when the three higher varnas are there to support him? Why need the Shudra bother to take to education, when there is the Brahmin to whom he can go when the occasion for reading or writing arises? Why need the Shudra worry to arm himself, when there is the Kshatriya to protect him? The theory of chaturvarnya, understood in this sense, may be said to look upon the Shudra as the ward and the three higher varnas as his guardians. Thus interpreted, it is a simple, elevating, and alluring theory.

Assuming this to be the correct view of the underlying conception of chaturvarnya, it seems to me that the system is neither foolproof nor knave- proof. What is to happen if the Brahmins, Vaishyas, and Kshatriyas fail to pursue knowledge, to engage in economic enterprise, and to be efficient soldiers, which are their respective functions? Contrary-wise, suppose that they discharge their functions, but flout their duty to the Shudra or to one another; what is to happen to the Shudra if the three classes refuse to support him on fair terms, or combine to keep him down? Who is to safeguard the interests of the Shudra—or for that matter, those of the Vaishya and Kshatriya—when the person who is trying to take advantage of his ignorance is the Brahmin? Who is to defend the liberty of the Shudra—and for that matter, of the Brahmin and the Vaishya—when the person who is robbing him of it is the Kshatriya?

Interdependence of one class on another class is inevitable. Even dependence of one class upon another may sometimes become allowable. But why make one person depend upon another in the matter of his vital needs? Education, everyone must have. Means of defence, everyone must have. These are the paramount requirements of every man for his self-preservation. How can the fact that his neighbour is educated and armed help a man who is uneducated and disarmed? The whole theory is absurd. These are the questions which the defenders of chaturvarnya do not seem to be troubled about. But they are very pertinent questions. Assuming that in their conception of chaturvarnya the relationship between the different classes is that of ward and guardian, and that this is the real conception underlying chaturvarnya, it must be admitted that it makes no provision to safeguard the interests of the ward from the misdeeds of the guardian.

Whether or not the relationship of guardian and ward was the real underlying conception on which chaturvarnya was based, there is no doubt that in practice the relation was that of master and servants. The three classes, Brahmins, Kshatriyas and Vaishyas, although not very happy in their mutual relationship, managed to work by compromise. The Brahmin flattered the

Kshatriya, and both let the Vaishya live in order to be able to live upon him. But the three agreed to beat down the Shudra. He was not allowed to acquire wealth, lest he should be independent of the three varnas. He was prohibited from acquiring knowledge, lest he should keep a steady vigil regarding his interests. He was prohibited from bearing arms, lest he should have the means to rebel against their authority. That this is how the Shudras were treated by the *tryavarnikas* is evidenced by the laws of Manu. There is no code of laws more infamous regarding social rights than the laws of Manu. Any instance from anywhere of social injustice must pale before it.

Why have the mass of people tolerated the social evils to which they have been subjected? There have been social revolutions in other countries of the world. Why have there not been social revolutions in India, is a question which has incessantly troubled me. There is only one answer which I can give, and it is that the lower classes of Hindus have been completely disabled for direct action on account of this wretched caste system. They could not bear arms, and without arms they could not rebel. They were all ploughmen—or rather, condemned to be ploughmen—and they never were allowed to convert their ploughshares into swords. They had no bayonets, and therefore everyone who chose, could and did sit upon them. On account of the caste system, they could receive no education. They could not think out or know the way to their salvation. They were condemned to be lowly; and not knowing the way of escape, and not having the means of escape, they became reconciled to eternal servitude, which they accepted as their inescapable fate.

It is true that even in Europe the strong have not shrunk from the exploitation—nay, the spoliation—of the weak. But in Europe, the strong have never contrived to make the weak helpless against exploitation so shamelessly as was the case in India among the Hindus. Social war has been raging between the strong and the weak far more violently in Europe than it has ever been in India. Yet the weak in Europe has had in his freedom of military service, his physical weapon; in suffering, his political weapon; and in education, his moral weapon. These three weapons for emancipation were never withheld by the strong from the weak in Europe. All these weapons were, however, denied to the masses in India by the caste system.

There cannot be a more degrading system of social organisation than the caste system. It is the system which deadens, paralyses, and cripples the people, from helpful activity. This is no exaggeration. History bears ample evidence. There is only one period in Indian history which is a period of freedom, greatness and glory. That is the period of the Maurya empire. At all other times the country suffered from defeat and darkness. But the Maurya period was a period when the caste system was completely annihilated—when the Shudras, who constituted the mass of the people, came into their own and became the rulers of the country. The period of defeat and darkness is the period when the caste system flourished, to the damnation of the greater part of the people of the country.

* * * * * *

Chaturvarnya is not new. It is as old as the Vedas. That is one of the reasons why we are asked by the Arya Samajists to consider its claims. Judging from the past, as a system of social organisation it has been tried, and it has failed. How many times have the Brahmins annihilated the seed of the Kshatriyas! How many times have the Kshatriyas annihilated the Brahmins! The Mahabharata and the Puranas are full of incidents of the strife between the Brahmins and the Kshatriyas. They even quarrelled over such petty questions as to who should salute first, as to who should give way first, the Brahmins or the Kshatriyas, when the two met in the street.

Not only was the Brahmin an eyesore to the Kshatriya and the Kshatriya an eyesore to the Brahmin, it seems that the Kshatriyas had become tyrannical, and the masses, disarmed as they were under the system of chaturvarnya, were praying to almighty god for relief from their tyranny. The Bhagwat tells us very definitely that Krishna had taken avatar for one sacred purpose: and that was, to annihilate the Kshatriyas. With these instances of rivalry and enmity between the different varnas before us, I do not understand how anyone can hold out chaturvarnya as an ideal to be aimed at, or as a pattern on which Hindu society should be remodelled.

******

I have dealt with those who are without you and whose hostility to your ideal is quite open. There appear to be others who are neither without you nor with you. I was hesitating whether I should deal with their point of view. But on further consideration I have come to the conclusion that I must, and that for two reasons. Firstly, their attitude to the problem of caste is not merely an attitude of neutrality, but is an attitude of armed neutrality. Secondly, they probably represent a considerable body of people. Of these, there is one set which finds nothing peculiar or odious in the caste system of the Hindus. Such Hindus cite the case of Muslims, Sikhs and Christians, and find comfort in the fact that they too have castes amongst them.

In considering this question, you must at the outset bear in mind that nowhere is human society one single whole. It is always plural. In the world of action, the individual is one limit and society the other. Between them lie all sorts of associative arrangements of lesser and larger scope—families, friendships, cooperative associations, business combines, political parties, bands of thieves and robbers. These small groups are usually firmly welded together, and are often as exclusive as castes. They have a narrow and intensive code, which is often anti-social. This is true of every society, in Europe as well as in Asia. The question to be asked in determining whether a given society is an ideal society is not whether there are groups in it, because groups exist in all societies.

The questions to be asked in determining what is an ideal society are: How numerous and varied are the interests which are consciously shared by the groups? How full and free is the interplay with other forms of associations? Are the forces that separate groups and classes more numerous than the forces that unite them? What social significance is attached to this group life? Is its exclusiveness a matter of custom and convenience, or is it a matter of religion? It is in the light of these questions that one must decide whether caste among non-Hindus is the same as caste among Hindus.

If we apply these considerations to castes among Mahomedans, Sikhs and Christians on the one hand, and to castes among Hindus on the other, you will find that caste among non-Hindus is fundamentally different from caste among Hindus. First, the ties which consciously make the Hindus hold together are non-existent, while among non-Hindus there are many that hold them together.

The strength of a society depends upon the presence of points of contact, possibilities of interaction, between different groups which exist in it. These are what Carlyle calls "organic filaments"—i.e., the elastic threads which help to bring the disintegrating elements together and to reunite them. There is no integrating force among the Hindus to counteract the disintegration caused by caste. While among the non-Hindus there are plenty of these "organic filaments" which bind them together.

Again it must be borne in mind that although there are castes among non-Hindus, as there are among Hindus, caste has not the same social significance for non-Hindus as it has for Hindus. Ask a Mahomedan or a Sikh who he is. He tells you that he is a Mahomedan or a Sikh, as the case may be. He does not tell you his caste although he has one, and you are satisfied with his answer. When he tells you that he is a Muslim, you do not proceed to ask him whether he is a Shia or a Sunni; Sheikh or Saiyad; Khatik or Pinjari. When he tells you he is a Sikh, you do not ask him whether he is Jat or Roda; Mazbi or Ramdasi. But you are not satisfied if a person tells you that he is a Hindu. You feel bound to inquire into his caste. Why? Because so essential is caste in the case of a Hindu that without knowing it you do not feel sure what sort of a being he is.

That caste has not the same social significance among non-Hindus as it has among Hindus is clear, if you take into consideration the consequences which follow breach of caste. There may be castes among Sikhs and Mahomedans, but the Sikhs and the Mahomedans will not outcast a Sikh or a Mahomedan if he broke his caste. Indeed, the very idea of excommunication is foreign to the Sikhs and the Mahomedans. But with the Hindus the case is entirely different. A Hindu is sure to be outcasted if he broke caste. This shows the difference in the social significance of caste to Hindus and non-Hindus. This is the second point of difference.

But there is also a third and a more important one. Caste among the non-Hindus has no religious consecration; but among the Hindus most decidedly it has. Among the non-Hindus, caste is only a practice, not a sacred institution. They did not originate it. With them it is only a survival mechanism. They do not regard caste as a religious dogma. Religion compels the Hindus to treat isolation and segregation of castes as a virtue. Religion does not compel the non-Hindus to take the same attitude towards caste. If Hindus wish to break caste, their religion will come in their way. But it will not be so in the case of non-Hindus. It is, therefore, a dangerous delusion to take comfort in the mere existence of caste among non-Hindus, without caring to know what place caste occupies in their life and whether there are other "organic filaments" which subordinate the feeling of caste to the feeling of community. The sooner the Hindus are cured of this delusion, the better.

The other set denies that caste presents any problem at all for the Hindus to consider. Such Hindus seek comfort in the view that the Hindus have survived, and take this as a proof of their fitness to survive. This point of view is well expressed by Prof S. Radhakrishnan in his *Hindu View of Life*. Referring to Hinduism, he says:

> The civilisation itself has not been a short-lived one. Its historic records date back to over four thousand years and

even then it had reached a stage of civilisation which has continued its unbroken, though at times slow and static, course until the present day. It has stood the stress and strain of more than four or five millenniums of spiritual thought and experience. Though peoples of different races and cultures have been pouring into India from the dawn of history, Hinduism has been able to maintain its supremacy and even the proselytising creeds backed by political power have not been able to coerce the large majority of Hindus to their views. The Hindu culture possesses some vitality which seems to be denied to some other more forceful currents. It is no more necessary to dissect Hinduism than to open a tree to see whether the sap still runs.

The name of Prof Radhakrishnan is big enough to invest with profundity whatever he says, and impress the minds of his readers. But I must not hesitate to speak out my mind. For I fear that his statement may become the basis of a vicious argument that the fact of survival is proof of fitness to survive.

It seems to me that the question is not whether a community lives or dies; the question is on what plane does it live. There are different modes of survival. But not all are equally honourable. For an individual as well as for a society, there is a gulf between merely living, and living worthily. To fight in a battle and to live in glory is one mode. To beat a retreat, to surrender, and to live the life of a captive is also a mode of survival. It is useless for a Hindu to take comfort in the fact that he and his people have survived. What he must consider is, what is the quality of their survival. If he does that, I am sure he will cease to take pride in the mere fact of survival. A Hindu's life has been a life of continuous defeat, and what appears to him to be life everlasting is not living everlastingly, but is really a life which is perishing everlastingly. It is a mode of survival of which every right-minded Hindu who is not afraid to own up to the truth will feel ashamed.

* * * * * *

There is no doubt, in my opinion, that unless you change your social order you can achieve little by way of progress. You cannot mobilise the community either for defence or for offence. You cannot build anything on the foundations of caste. You cannot build up a nation, you cannot build up a morality. Anything that you will build on the foundations of caste will crack, and will never be a whole.

The only question that remains to be considered is—How to bring about the reform of the Hindu social order? How to abolish caste? This is a question of supreme importance. There is a view that in the reform of caste, the first step to take is to abolish sub-castes. This view is based upon the supposition that there is a greater similarity in manners and status between sub-castes than there is between castes. I think this is an erroneous supposition. The Brahmins of northern and central India are socially of lower grade, as compared with the Brahmins of the Deccan and southern India. The former are only cooks and water-carriers, while the latter occupy a high social position. On the other hand, in northern India, the Vaishyas and Kayasthas are intellectually and socially on a par with the Brahmins of the Deccan and southern India.

Again, in the matter of food there is no similarity between the Brahmins of the Deccan and southern India, who are vegetarians, and the Brahmins of Kashmere and Bengal, who are non-vegetarians. On the other hand, the Brahmins of the Deccan and southern India have more in common so far as food is concerned with such non-Brahmins as the Gujaratis, Marwaris, Banias and Jains.

There is no doubt that from the standpoint of making the transition from one caste to another easy, the fusion of the Kayasthas of northern India and the other non-Brahmins of southern India with the non-Brahmins of the Deccan and the Dravidian country is more practicable than the fusion of the Brahmins of the south with the Brahmins of the north. But assuming that the fusion of sub-castes is possible, what guarantee is there that the abolition of sub-castes will necessarily lead to the abolition of castes? On the contrary, it may happen that the process may stop with the abolition of sub-castes. In that case, the abolition of sub-castes will only help to strengthen the castes, and make them more powerful and therefore more mischievous. This remedy is therefore neither practicable nor effective, and may easily prove to be a wrong remedy.

Another plan of action for the abolition of caste is to begin with inter-caste dinners. This also, in my opinion, is an inadequate remedy. There are many castes which allow inter-dining. But it is a common experience that inter- dining has not succeeded in killing the spirit of caste and the consciousness of caste. I am convinced that the real remedy is intermarriage. Fusion of blood can alone create the feeling of being kith and kin, and unless this feeling of kinship, of being kindred, becomes paramount, the separatist feeling—the feeling of being aliens—created by caste will not vanish. Among the Hindus, intermarriage must necessarily be a factor of greater force in social life than it need be in the life of the non-Hindus. Where society is already well knit by other ties, marriage is an ordinary incident of life.

But where society is cut asunder, marriage as a binding force becomes a matter of urgent necessity. The real remedy for breaking caste is intermarriage. Nothing else will serve as the solvent of caste.

Your Jat-Pat Todak Mandal has adopted this line of attack. It is a direct and frontal attack, and I congratulate you upon a correct diagnosis, and more upon your having shown the courage to tell the Hindus what is really wrong with them. Political tyranny is nothing compared to social tyranny, and a reformer who defies society is a much more courageous man than a politician who defies the government. You are right in holding that caste will cease to be an operative force only when inter-dining and intermarriage have become matters of common course. You have located the source of the disease.

But is your prescription the right prescription for the disease? Ask yourselves this question: Why is it that a large majority of Hindus do not inter-dine and do not intermarry? Why is it that your cause is not popular?

There can be only one answer to this question, and it is that interdining and intermarriage are repugnant to the beliefs and dogmas which the Hindus regard as sacred. Caste is not a physical object like a wall of bricks or a line of barbed wire which prevents the Hindus from commingling and which has, therefore, to be pulled down. Caste is a notion; it is a state of mind. The destruction of caste does not therefore mean the destruction of a physical barrier. It means a notional change.

Caste may be bad. Caste may lead to conduct so gross as to be called man's inhumanity to man. All the same, it must be recognised that the Hindus observe caste not because they are inhuman or wrong-headed. They observe caste because they are deeply religious. People are not wrong in observing caste. In my view, what is wrong is their religion, which has inculcated this notion of caste. If this is correct, then obviously the enemy you must grapple with is not the people who observe caste, but the shastras which teach them this religion of caste. Criticising and ridiculing people for not inter-dining or intermarrying, or occasionally holding inter-caste dinners and celebrating inter-caste marriages, is a futile method of achieving the desired end. The real remedy is to destroy the belief in the sanctity of the shastras.

How do you expect to succeed if you allow the shastras to continue to mould the beliefs and opinions of the people? Not to question the authority of the shastras—to permit the people to believe in their sanctity and their sanctions, and then to blame the people and to criticise them for their acts as being irrational and inhuman—is an incongruous way of carrying on social reform. Reformers working for the removal of untouchability, including Mahatma Gandhi, do not seem to realise that the acts of the people are merely the results of their beliefs inculcated in their minds by the shastras, and that people will not change their conduct until they cease to believe in the sanctity of the shastras on which their conduct is founded.

No wonder that such efforts have not produced any results. You also seem to be erring in the same way as the reformers working in the cause of removing untouchability. To agitate for and to organise inter-caste dinners and inter-caste marriages is like forced feeding brought about by artificial means. Make every man and woman free from the thraldom of the shastras, cleanse their minds of the pernicious notions founded on the shastras, and he or she will inter-dine and intermarry, without your telling him or her to do so.

It is no use seeking refuge in quibbles. It is no use telling people that the shastras do not say what they are believed to say, if they are grammatically read or logically interpreted. What matters is how the shastras have been understood by the people. You must take the stand that Buddha took. You must take the stand which Guru Nanak took. You must not only discard the shastras, you must deny their authority, as did Buddha and Nanak. You must have courage to tell the Hindus that what is wrong with them is their religion—the religion which has produced in them this notion of the sacredness of caste. Will you show that courage?

* * * * * *

What are your chances of success? Social reforms fall into different species. There is a species of reform which does not relate to the religious notions of a people, but is purely secular in character. There is also a species of reform which relates to the religious notions of a people. Of such a species of reform, there are two varieties. In one, the reform accords with the principles of the religion, and merely invites people who have departed from it, to revert to them and to follow them.

The second is a reform which not only touches the religious principles but is diametrically opposed to those principles, and invites people to depart from and to discard their authority, and to act contrary to those principles. Caste is the natural outcome of certain religious beliefs which have the sanction of the shastras, which are believed to contain the command of divinely inspired sages who were endowed with a supernatural wisdom and whose commands, therefore, cannot be disobeyed without committing a sin.

The destruction of caste is a reform which falls under the third category. To ask people to give up caste is to ask them to go contrary to their fundamental religious notions. It is obvious that the first and second species of reform are easy. But the third is a stupendous task, well-nigh impossible. The Hindus hold to the sacredness of the social order. Caste has a divine basis. You must therefore destroy the sacredness and divinity with which caste has become invested. In the last analysis, this means you must destroy the authority of the shastras and the Vedas.

I have emphasised this question of the ways and means of destroying caste, because I think that knowing the proper ways and means is more important than knowing the ideal. If you do not know the real ways and means, all your shots are sure to be misfired. If my analysis is correct, then your task is Herculean. You alone can say whether you are capable of achieving it.

Speaking for myself, I see the task to be well-nigh impossible. Perhaps you would like to know why I think so. Out of the many reasons which have led me to take this view, I will mention some which I regard as most important. One of these reasons is the attitude of hostility which the Brahmins have shown towards this question. The Brahmins form the vanguard of the movement for political reform, and in some cases also of economic reform. But they are not to be found even as camp-followers in the army raised to break down the barricades of caste. Is there any hope of the Brahmins ever taking up a lead in the future in this matter? I say no.

You may ask why. You may argue that there is no reason why Brahmins should continue to shun social reform. You may argue that the Brahmins know that the bane of Hindu society is caste, and as an enlightened class they could not be expected to be indifferent to its consequences. You may argue that there are secular Brahmins and priestly Brahmins, and if the latter do not take up the cudgels on behalf of those who want to break caste, the former will.

All this of course sounds very plausible. But in all this it is forgotten that the break-up of the caste system is bound to adversely affect the Brahmin caste. Having regard to this, is it reasonable to expect that the Brahmins will ever consent to lead a movement, the ultimate result of which is to destroy the power and prestige of the Brahmin caste? Is it reasonable to expect the secular Brahmins to take part in a movement directed against the priestly Brahmins? In my judgement, it is useless to make a distinction between the secular Brahmins and priestly Brahmins. Both are kith and kin. They are two arms of the same body, and one is bound to fight for the existence of the other.

In this connection, I am reminded of some very pregnant remarks made by Prof Dicey in his *English Constitution*. Speaking of the actual limitation on the legislative supremacy of parliament, Dicey says:

> The actual exercise of authority by any sovereign whatever, and notably by Parliament, is bounded or controlled by two limitations. Of these the one is an external, the other is an internal limitation. The external limit to the real power of a sovereign consists in the possibility or certainty that his subjects, or a large number of them, will disobey or resist his laws . . .
>
> The internal limit to the exercise of sovereignty arises from the nature of the sovereign power itself. Even a despot exercises his powers in accordance with his character, which is itself moulded by the circumstances under which he lives, including under that head the moral feelings of the time and the society to which he belongs. The Sultan could not, if he would, change the religion of the Mahommedan world,

but even if he could do so, it is in the very highest degree improbable that the head of Mahommedanism should wish to overthrow the religion of Mahomet; the internal check on the exercise of the Sultan's power is at least as strong as the external limitation. People sometimes ask the idle question, why the Pope does not introduce this or that reform? The true answer is that a revolutionist is not the kind of man who becomes a Pope, and that the man who becomes a Pope has no wish to be a revolutionist.

I think these remarks apply equally to the Brahmins of India, and one can say with equal truth that if a man who becomes a Pope has no wish to become a revolutionary, a man who is born a Brahmin has much less desire to become a revolutionary. Indeed, to expect a Brahmin to be a revolutionary in matters of social reform is as idle as to expect the British Parliament, as was said by Leslie Stephen, to pass an Act requiring all blue-eyed babies to be murdered.

Some of you will say that it is a matter of small concern whether the Brahmins come forward to lead the movement against caste or whether they do not. To take this view is, in my judgement, to ignore the part played by the intellectual class in the community. Whether you accept the theory of the great man as the maker of history or whether you do not, this much you will have to concede: that in every country the intellectual class is the most influential class, if not the governing class. The intellectual class is the class which can foresee, it is the class which can advise and give the lead. In no country does the mass of the people live the life of intelligent thought and action. It is largely imitative, and follows the intellectual class.

There is no exaggeration in saying that the entire destiny of a country depends upon its intellectual class. If the intellectual class is honest, independent and disinterested, it can be trusted to take the initiative and give a proper lead when a crisis arises. It is true that intellect by itself is no virtue. It is only a means, and the use of means depends upon the ends which an intellectual person pursues. An intellectual man can be a good man, but he can easily be a rogue. Similarly an intellectual class may be a band of high-souled persons, ready to help, ready to emancipate erring humanity—or it may easily be a gang of crooks, or a body of advocates for a narrow clique from which it draws its support.

You may think it a pity that the intellectual class in India is simply another name for the Brahmin caste. You may regret that the two are one; that the existence of the intellectual class should be bound up with one single caste; that this intellectual class should share the interest and the aspirations of that Brahmin caste, which has regarded itself as the custodian of the interest of that caste rather than of the interests of the country. All this may be very regrettable. But the fact remains that the Brahmins form the intellectual class of the Hindus. It is not only an intellectual class, but it is a class which is held in great reverence by the rest of the Hindus.

The Hindus are taught that the Brahmins are *Bhu-devas* (gods on earth).

वर्णानाम ब्राह्मणों गुरु The Hindus are taught that Brahmins alone can be their teachers. Manu says:

> If it be asked how it should be with respect to points of the Dharma which have not been specially mentioned, the answer is, that which Brahmins who are *shishthas* propound shall doubtless have legal force.

अनाम्नातेषु धर्मेषु कथं स्यादिति चेद्भवेत्।
यं शिष्टा बाह्मणा ब्रूयुः स धर्म स्यादशङ्कितः।।

When such an intellectual class, which holds the rest of the community in its grip, is opposed to the reform of caste, the chances of success in a movement for the break-up of the caste system appear to me very, very remote.

The second reason why I say the task is impossible will be clear, if you will bear in mind that the caste system has two aspects. In one of its aspects, it divides men into separate communities. In its second aspect, it places these communities in a graded order one above the other in social status. Each caste takes its pride and its consolation in the fact that in the scale of castes it is above some other caste. As an outward mark of this gradation, there is also a gradation of social and religious rights, technically spoken of as *ashtadhikaras* and *sanskaras*. The higher the grade of a caste, the greater the number of these rights; and the lower the grade, the lesser their number.

Now this gradation, this scaling of castes, makes it impossible to organise a common front against the caste system. If a caste claims the right to inter-dine and intermarry with another caste placed above it, it is frozen the instant it is told by mischief-mongers—and there are many Brahmins amongst such mischief-mongers—that it will have to concede inter-dining and intermarriage with castes below it! All are slaves of the caste system. But all the slaves are not equal in status.

To excite the proletariat to bring about an economic revolution, Karl Marx told them: "You have nothing to lose except your chains." But the artful way in which the social and religious rights are distributed among the different castes, whereby some have more and some have less, makes the slogan of Karl Marx quite useless to excite the Hindus against the caste system. Castes form a graded system of sovereignties, high and low, which are jealous of their status and which know that if a general dissolution came, some of them stand to lose more of their prestige and power than others do. You cannot, therefore, have a general mobilisation of the Hindus (to use a military expression) for an attack on the caste system.

Can you appeal to reason, and ask the Hindus to discard caste as being contrary to reason? That raises the question: Is a Hindu free to follow his reason? Manu has laid down three sanctions to which every Hindu must conform in the matter of his behaviour:

वेदः स्म्रितिः सदाचारः च प्रियमात्मनः

Here there is no place for reason to play its part. A Hindu must follow either Veda, smriti or *sadachar.* He cannot follow anything else.

In the first place, how are the texts of the Vedas and smritis to be interpreted whenever any doubt arises regarding their meaning? On this important question the view of Manu is quite definite. He says:

योऽवमन्येत ते मूले हेतुशास्त्राश्रयाद्द्विजः।
स साधुभिर्बहिष्कार्यो नास्तिको वेदनिन्दकः॥

According to this rule, rationalism as a canon of interpreting the Vedas and smritis is absolutely condemned. It is regarded to be as wicked as atheism, and the punishment provided for it is excommunication. Thus, where a matter is covered by the Veda or the smriti, a Hindu cannot resort to rational thinking.

Even when there is a conflict between Vedas and smritis on matters on which they have given a positive injunction, the solution is not left to reason. When there is a conflict between two shrutis, both are to be regarded as of equal authority. Either of them may be followed. No attempt is to be made to find out which of the two accords with reason. This is made clear by Manu:

श्रुतिद्वैधं तु यत्र स्यात्तत्र धर्मावुभौ स्मृतौ।

When there is a conflict between shruti and smriti, the shruti must prevail. But here too no attempt must be made to find out which of the two accords with reason. This is laid down by Manu in the following shloka:

या वेदवावाह्या: स्मृतयो याश्च काश्च कुदृष्टयः।
सर्वास्ता निष्फला: प्रेत्य तमोनिष्ठा हि ता: स्मृता:॥

Again, when there is a conflict between two smritis, the *Manusmriti* must prevail, but no attempt is to be made to find out which of the two accords with reason. This is the ruling given by Brihaspati:

वेदार्थत्वोपनिबंधृत्बात प्रामाण्यं हि मनो: स्म्रितं।
मन्वर्थविपरीता तु या स्मृति: सा न शस्यते॥

It is therefore clear that in any matter on which the shrutis and smritis have given a positive direction, a Hindu is not free to use his reasoning faculty. The same rule is laid down in the Mahabharata:

पुराणं मानवो धर्मः सांगो वेदश्चिकित्सितं।
आज्ञासिद्धानि चत्वारि न हन्तव्यानि हेतुभिः॥

He must abide by their directions. Caste and varna are matters which are dealt with by the Vedas and the smritis, and consequently, appeal to reason can have no effect on a Hindu.

So far as caste and varna are concerned, not only the shastras do not permit the Hindu to use his reason in the decision of the question, but they have taken care to see that no occasion is left to examine in a rational way the foundations of his belief in caste and varna. It must be a source of silent amusement to many a non-Hindu to find hundreds and thousands of Hindus breaking caste on certain occasions, such as railway journeys and foreign travel, and yet endeavouring to maintain caste for the rest of their lives!

The explanation of this phenomenon discloses another fetter on the reasoning faculties of the Hindus. Man's life is generally habitual and unreflective. Reflective thought—in the sense of active, persistent, and careful consideration of any belief or supposed form of knowledge, in the light of the grounds that support it and the further conclusions to which it tends—is quite rare, and arises only in a situation which presents a dilemma or a crisis. Railway journeys and foreign travels are really occasions of crisis in the life of a Hindu, and it is natural to expect a Hindu to ask himself why he should maintain caste at all, if he cannot maintain it at all times. But he does not.

He breaks caste at one step, and proceeds to observe it at the next, without raising any question.

The reason for this astonishing conduct is to be found in the rule of the shastras, which directs him to maintain caste as far as possible and to undergo *prayaschitta* when he cannot. By this theory of prayaschitta, the shastras, by following a spirit of compromise, have given caste a perpetual lease on life, and have smothered the reflective thought which would have otherwise led to the destruction of the notion of caste.

There have been many who have worked in the cause of the abolition of caste and untouchability. Of those who can be mentioned, Ramanuja, Kabir, and others stand out prominently. Can you appeal to the acts of these reformers and exhort the Hindus to follow them?

It is true that Manu has included सदाचार (sadachar) as one of the sanctions along with shruti and smriti. Indeed, sadachar has been given a higher place than shastras:

यद्यदाचर्यते येन धर्म्यं वाऽधर्म्यमेव वा।
देशस्याचरणं नित्यं चरित्रं तद्धिकीर्तितम्।।

According to this, sadachar, whether it is धर्म्य or अधर्म्य in accordance with shastras or contrary to shastras, must be followed. But what is the meaning of sadachar? If anyone were to suppose that sadachar means right or good acts— i.e., acts of good and righteous men— he would find himself greatly mistaken. Sadachar does not mean good acts or acts of good men. It means ancient custom, good or bad. The following verse makes this clear:

यस्मिन देशे य आचार: पारंपर्यक्रमागत।
वर्णानां किल सर्वेषां स सदाचार उच्यते।।

As though to warn people against the view that sadachar means good acts or acts of good men, and fearing that people might understand it that way and follow the acts of good men, the smritis have commanded the Hindus in unmistakable terms not to follow even gods in their good deeds, if they are contrary to shruti, smriti and sadachar. This may sound to be most extraordinary, most perverse, but the fact remains that न देवचरितमं चरेत् is an injunction issued to the Hindus by their shastras.

Reason and morality are the two most powerful weapons in the armoury of a reformer. To deprive him of the use of these weapons is to disable him for action. How are you going to break up caste, if people are not free to consider whether it accords with reason? How are you going to break up caste, if people are not free to consider whether it accords with morality? The wall built around caste is impregnable, and the material of which it is built contains none of the combustible stuff of reason and morality. Add to this the fact that inside this wall stands the army of Brahmins who form the intellectual class, Brahmins who are the natural leaders of the Hindus, Brahmins who are there not as mere mercenary soldiers but as an army fighting for its homeland, and you will get an idea why I think that the breaking up of caste among the Hindus is well-nigh impossible. At any rate, it would take ages before a breach is made.

But whether the doing of the deed takes time or whether it can be done quickly, you must not forget that if you wish to bring about a breach in the system, then you have got to apply the dynamite to the Vedas and the shastras, which deny any part to reason; to the Vedas and shastras, which deny any part to morality. You must destroy the religion of the shrutis and the smritis. Nothing else will avail. This is my considered view of the matter.

Some may not understand what I mean by destruction of religion, some may find the idea revolting to them, and some may find it revolutionary. Let me therefore explain my position. I do not know whether you draw a distinction between principles and rules. But I do. Not only do I make a distinction, but I say that this distinction is real and important. Rules are practical; they are habitual ways of doing things according to prescription. But principles are intellectual; they are useful methods of judging things. Rules seek to tell an agent just what course of action to pursue. Principles do not prescribe a specific course of action. Rules, like cooking recipes, do tell just what to do and how to do it. A principle, such as that of justice, supplies a main heading by reference to which he is to consider the bearings of his desires and purposes; it guides him in his thinking by suggesting to him the important consideration which he should bear in mind.

This difference between rules and principles makes the acts done in pursuit of them different in quality and in content. Doing what is said to be good by virtue of a rule and doing good in the light of a principle are two different things. The principle may be wrong, but the act is conscious and responsible. The rule may be right, but the act is mechanical. A religious act may not be a correct act, but must at least be a responsible act. To permit of this responsibility, religion must mainly be a matter of principles only. It cannot be a matter of rules. The moment it degenerates into rules it ceases to be religion, as it kills the responsibility which is the essence of a truly religious act.

What is this Hindu religion? Is it a set of principles, or is it a code of rules? Now the Hindu religion, as contained in the Vedas and the smritis, is nothing but a mass of sacrificial, social, political, and sanitary rules and regulations, all mixed up. What is called religion by the Hindus is nothing but a multitude of commands and prohibitions. Religion, in the sense of spiritual principles, truly universal, applicable to all races, to all countries, to all times, is not to be found in them; and if it is, it does not form the governing part of a Hindu's life. That for a Hindu dharma means commands and prohibitions is clear from the way the word dharma is used in the Vedas and the smritis and understood by the commentators. The word dharma as used in the Vedas in most cases means religious ordinances or rites. Even Jaimini in his *Purva Mimamsa* defines dharma as "a desirable goal or result that is indicated by injunctive (Vedic) passages".

To put it in plain language, what the Hindus call religion is really law, or at best legalised class-ethics. Frankly, I refuse to call this code of ordinances as religion. The first evil of such a code of ordinances, misrepresented to the people as religion, is that it tends to deprive moral life of freedom and spontaneity, and to reduce it (for the conscientious, at any rate) to a more or less anxious and servile conformity to externally imposed rules.

Under it, there is no loyalty to ideals; there is only conformity to commands.

But the worst evil of this code of ordinances is that the laws it contains must be the same yesterday, today and forever. They are iniquitous in that they are not the same for one class as for another. But this iniquity is made perpetual in that they are prescribed to be the same for all generations. The objectionable part of such a scheme is not that they are made by certain persons called prophets or law-givers. The objectionable part is that this code has been invested with the character of finality and fixity. Happiness notoriously varies with the conditions and circumstances of a person, as well as with the conditions of different people and epochs. That being the case, how can humanity endure this code of eternal laws, without being cramped and without being crippled?

I have, therefore, no hesitation in saying that such a religion must be destroyed, and I say there is nothing irreligious in working for the destruction of such a religion. Indeed, I hold that it is your bounden duty to tear off the mask, to remove the misrepresentation that is caused by misnaming this law as religion. This is an essential step for you. Once you clear the minds of the people of this misconception and enable them to realise that what they are told is religion is not religion, but that it is really law, you will be in a position to urge its amendment or abolition.

So long as people look upon it as religion they will not be ready for a change, because the idea of religion is generally speaking not associated with the idea of change. But the idea of law is associated with the idea of change, and when people come to know that what is called religion is really law, old and archaic, they will be ready for a change, for people know and accept that law can be changed.

* * * * * *

While I condemn a religion of rules, I must not be understood to hold the opinion that there is no necessity for a religion. On the contrary, I agree with Burke when he says that "True religion is the foundation of society, the basis on which all true Civil Government rests, and both their sanction." Consequently, when I urge that these ancient rules of life be annulled, I am anxious that their place shall be taken by a religion of principles, which alone can lay claim to being a true religion. Indeed, I am so convinced of the necessity of religion that I feel I ought to tell you in outline what I regard as necessary items in this religious reform. The following, in my opinion, should be the cardinal items in this reform:

There should be one and only one standard book of Hindu religion, acceptable to all Hindus and recognised by all Hindus. This of course means that all other books of Hindu religion such as Vedas, shastras, and puranas, which are treated as sacred and authoritative, must by law cease to be so, and the preaching of any doctrine, religious or social, contained in these books should be penalised.

It would be better if priesthood among Hindus were abolished. But as this seems to be impossible, the priesthood must at least cease to be hereditary. Every person who professes to be a Hindu must be eligible for being a priest. It should be provided by law that no Hindu shall be entitled to be a priest unless he has passed an examination prescribed by the state, and holds a *sanad* from the state permitting him to practise.

No ceremony performed by a priest who does not hold a sanad shall be deemed to be valid in law, and it should be made penal for a person who has no sanad to officiate as a priest.

A priest should be the servant of the state, and should be subject to the disciplinary action of the state in the matter of his morals, beliefs, and worship, in addition to his being subject along with other citizens to the ordinary law of the land.

The number of priests should be limited by law according to the requirements of the state, as is done in the case of the ICS [Indian Civil Service].

To some, this may sound radical. But to my mind there is nothing revolutionary in this. Every profession in India is regulated. Engineers must show proficiency, doctors must show proficiency, lawyers must show proficiency, before they are allowed to practise their professions. During the whole of their career, they must not only obey the law of the land, civil as well as criminal, but they must also obey the special code of morals prescribed by their respective professions. The priest's is the only profession where proficiency is not required. The profession of a Hindu priest is the only profession which is not subject to any code.

Mentally a priest may be an idiot, physically a priest may be suffering from a foul disease such as syphilis or gonorrhoea, morally he may be a wreck. But he is fit to officiate at solemn ceremonies, to enter the *sanctum sanctorum* of a Hindu temple, and to worship the Hindu god. All this becomes possible among the Hindus because for a priest it is enough to be born in a priestly caste. The whole thing is abominable, and is due to the fact that the priestly class among Hindus is subject neither to law nor to morality. It recognises no duties. It knows only of rights and privileges. It is a pest which divinity seems to have let loose on the masses for their mental and moral degradation.

The priestly class must be brought under control by some such legislation as I have outlined above. This will prevent it from doing mischief and from misguiding people. It will democratise it by throwing it open to everyone. It will certainly help to kill Brahminism and will also help to kill caste, which is nothing but Brahminism incarnate. Brahminism is the poison which has spoiled Hinduism. You will succeed in saving Hinduism if you will kill Brahminism. There should be no opposition to this reform from any quarter. It should be welcomed even by the

Arya Samajists, because this is merely an application of their own doctrine of guna-karma.

Whether you do that or you do not, you must give a new doctrinal basis to your religion—a basis that will be in consonance with liberty, equality and fraternity; in short, with democracy. I am no authority on the subject. But I am told that for such religious principles as will be in consonance with liberty, equality and fraternity, it may not be necessary for you to borrow from foreign sources, and that you could draw for such principles on the Upanishads. Whether you could do so without a complete remoulding, a considerable scraping and chipping off from the ore they contain, is more than I can say. This means a complete change in the fundamental notions of life. It means a complete change in the values of life. It means a complete change in outlook and in attitude towards men and things.

It means conversion; but if you do not like the word, I will say it means new life. But a new life cannot enter a body that is dead. New life can enter only into a new body. The old body must die before a new body can come into existence and a new life can enter into it. To put it simply: the old must cease to be operative before the new can begin to enliven and to pulsate. This is what I meant when I said you must discard the authority of the shastras, and destroy the religion of the shastras.

I have kept you too long. It is time I brought this address to a close. This would have been a convenient point for me to have stopped. But this would probably be my last address to a Hindu audience, on a subject vitally concerning the Hindus. I would therefore like, before I close, to place before the Hindus, if they will allow me, some questions which I regard as vital, and invite them seriously to consider the same.

In the first place, the Hindus must consider whether it is sufficient to take the placid view of the anthropologist that there is nothing to be said about the beliefs, habits, morals and outlooks on life which obtain among the different peoples of the world, except that they often differ; or whether it is not necessary to make an attempt to find out what kind of morality, beliefs, habits, and outlook have worked best and have enabled those who possessed them to flourish, to grow strong, to people the earth and to have dominion over it. As is observed by Professor Carver:

> [M]orality and religion, as the organised expression of moral approval and disapproval, must be regarded as factors in the struggle for existence as truly as are weapons for offence and defence, teeth and claws, horns and hoofs, fur and feathers, plumage, beards, and antlers. The social group, community, tribe or nation which develops an unworkable scheme of morality, or within which those social acts which weaken it and unfit it for survival habitually create the sentiment of approval, while those which would strengthen it and enable it to expand habitually create the sentiment of disapproval, will eventually be eliminated. Its habits of approval and disapproval handicap it as really as the possession of two wings on one side with none on the other would handicap a colony of flies. It would be as futile in one case as in the other to argue that one system was just as good as another.

Morality and religion, therefore, are not mere matters of likes and dislikes. You may dislike exceedingly a scheme of morality which, if universally practised within a nation, would make that nation the strongest nation on the face of the earth. Yet in spite of your dislike, such a nation will become strong. You may like exceedingly a scheme of morality and an ideal of justice which, if universally practised within a nation, would make it unable to hold its own in the struggle with other nations. Yet in spite of your admiration, this nation will eventually disappear. The Hindus must, therefore, examine their religion and their morality in terms of their survival value.

Secondly, the Hindus must consider whether they should conserve the whole of their social heritage, or select what is helpful and transmit to future generations only that much and no more. Prof John Dewey, who was my teacher and to whom I owe so much, has said:

> Every society gets encumbered with what is trivial, with dead wood from the past, and with what is positively perverse ... As a society becomes more enlightened, it realises that it is responsible not to conserve and transmit the whole of its existing achievements, but only such as make for a better future society.

Even Burke, in spite of the vehemence with which he opposed the principle of change embodied in the French Revolution, was compelled to admit that

> a State without the means of some change is without the means of its conservation. Without such means it might even risk the loss of that part of the constitution which it wished the most religiously to preserve.

What Burke said of a state applies equally to society.

Thirdly, the Hindus must consider whether they must not cease to worship the past as supplying their ideals. The baneful effects of this worship of the past are best summed up by Prof Dewey when he says:

> An individual can live only in the present. The present is not just something which comes after the past; much less something produced by it. It is what life is in leaving the past behind it. The study of past products will not help us to understand the present. A knowledge of the past and its heritage is of great significance when it enters into the present, but not otherwise. And the mistake of making the records and remains of the past the main material of education is that it tends to make the past a rival of the present and the present a more or less futile imitation of the past.

The principle, which makes little of the present act of living and growing, naturally looks upon the present as empty and upon the future as remote. Such a principle is inimical to progress and is a hindrance to a strong and a steady current of life.

Fourthly, the Hindus must consider whether the time has not come for them to recognise that there is nothing fixed, nothing eternal, nothing sanatan; that everything is changing, that change is the law of life for individuals as well as for society. In a changing society, there must be a constant revolution of old values; and the Hindus must realise that if there must be standards to measure the acts of men, there must also be a readiness to revise those standards.

* * * * * *

I have to confess that this address has become too lengthy. Whether this fault is compensated to any extent by breadth or depth is a matter for you to judge. All I claim is to have told you candidly my views. I have little to recommend them but some study and a deep concern in your destiny. If you will allow me to say it, these views are the views of a man who has been no tool of power, no flatterer of greatness. They come from one, almost the whole of whose public exertion has been one continuous struggle for liberty for the poor and for the oppressed, and whose only reward has been a continuous shower of calumny and abuse from national journals and national leaders, for no other reason except that I refuse to join with them in performing the miracle—I will not say trick—of liberating the oppressed with the gold of the tyrant, and raising the poor with the cash of the rich.

All this may not be enough to commend my views. I think they are not likely to alter yours. But whether they do or do not, the responsibility is entirely yours. You must make your efforts to uproot caste, if not in my way, then in your way.

I am sorry, I will not be with you. I have decided to change. This is not the place for giving reasons. But even when I am gone out of your fold, I will watch your movement with active sympathy, and you will have my assistance for what it may be worth. Yours is a national cause. Caste is no doubt primarily the breath of the Hindus. But the Hindus have fouled the air all over, and everybody is infected—Sikh, Muslim and Christian. You, therefore, deserve the support of all those who are suffering from this infection—Sikh, Muslim and Christian.

Yours is more difficult than the other national cause, namely, swaraj. In the fight for swaraj you fight with the whole nation on your side. In this, you have to fight against the whole nation—and that too, your own. But it is more important than swaraj. There is no use having swaraj, if you cannot defend it. More important than the question of defending swaraj is the question of defending the Hindus under the swaraj. In my opinion, it is only when Hindu society becomes a casteless society that it can hope to have strength enough to defend itself. Without such internal strength, swaraj for Hindus may turn out to be only a step towards slavery. Goodbye, and good wishes for your success.

A VINDICATION OF CASTE BY MAHATMA GANDHI

DR AMBEDKAR'S–INDICTMENT–1

The readers will recall the fact that Dr Ambedkar was to have presided last May at the annual conference of the Jat-Pat Todak Mandal of Lahore. But the conference itself was cancelled because Dr Ambedkar's address was found by the reception committee to be unacceptable. How far a reception committee is justified in rejecting a president of its choice because of his address that may be objectionable to it is open to question. The committee knew Dr Ambedkar's views on caste and the Hindu scriptures. They knew also that he had in unequivocal terms decided to give up Hinduism. Nothing less than the address that Dr Ambedkar had prepared was to be expected from him. The committee appears to have deprived the public of an opportunity of listening to the original views of a man who has carved out for himself a unique position in society. Whatever label he wears in future, Dr Ambedkar is not the man to allow himself to be forgotten.

Dr Ambedkar was not going to be beaten by the reception committee. He has answered their rejection of him by publishing the address at his own expense. He has priced it at 8 annas, I would suggest a reduction to 2 annas or at least 4 annas.

No reformer can ignore the address. The orthodox will gain by reading it. This is not to say that the address is not open to objection. It has to be read only because it is open to serious objection. Dr Ambedkar is a challenge to Hinduism. Brought up as a Hindu, 3 educated by a Hindu potentate, 4 he has become so disgusted with the so-called savarna Hindus or the treatment that he and his people have received at their hands that he proposes to leave not only them but the very religion that is his and their common heritage. He has transferred to that religion his disgust against a part of its professors.

But this is not to be wondered at. After all, one can only judge a system or an institution by the conduct of its representatives. What is more, Dr Ambedkar found that the vast majority of savarna Hindus had not only conducted themselves inhumanly against those of their fellow religionists whom they classed as Untouchables, but they had based their conduct on the authority of their scriptures, and when he began to search them, he had found ample warrant for their beliefs in untouchability and all its implications. The author of the address has quoted chapter and verse in proof of his three-fold indictment—inhuman conduct itself, the unabashed justification for it on the part of the perpetrators, and the subsequent discovery that the justification was warranted by their scriptures.

No Hindu who prizes his faith above life itself can afford to underrate the importance of this indictment. Dr Ambedkar is not alone in his disgust. He is its most uncompromising exponent and one of the ablest among them. He is certainly the most irreconcilable among them. Thank god, in the front rank of the leaders he is singularly alone, and as yet but a representative of a very small minority. But what he says is voiced with more or less vehemence by many leaders belonging to the Depressed Classes. Only the latter, for instance Rao Bahadur M.C. Rajah and Dewan Bahadur Srinivasan, 5 not only do not threaten to give up Hinduism, but find enough warmth in it to compensate for the shameful persecution to which the vast mass of Harijans are exposed.

But the fact of many leaders remaining in the Hindu fold is no warrant for disregarding what Dr Ambedkar has to say. The savarnas have to correct their belief and their conduct. Above all, those who are, by their learning and influence, among the savarnas have to give an authoritative interpretation of the scriptures. The questions that Dr Ambedkar's indictment suggests are:

1. What are the scriptures?
2. Are all the printed texts to be regarded as an integral part of them, or is any part of them to be rejected as unauthorised interpolation?
3. What is the answer of such accepted and expurgated scriptures on the question of untouchability, caste, equality of status, inter-dining and intermarriages? (These have been all examined by Dr Ambedkar in his address.)

I must reserve for the next issue my own answer to these questions and a statement of the (at least some) manifest flaws in Dr Ambedkar's thesis.

Harijan, 11 July 1936

DR AMBEDKAR'S INDICTMENT—2

The Vedas, Upanishads, smritis and puranas, including the Ramayana and the Mahabharata, are the Hindu scriptures. Nor is this a finite list. Every age or even generation has added to the list. It follows, therefore, that everything printed or even found handwritten is not scripture. The smritis, for instance, contain much that can never be accepted as the word of God. Thus many of the texts that Dr Ambedkar quotes from the smritis cannot be accepted as authentic. The scriptures, properly so called, can only be concerned with eternal verities and must appeal to any conscience, i.e., any heart whose eyes of understanding are opened. Nothing can be accepted as the word of God which cannot be tested by reason or be capable of being spiritually experienced. And even when you have an expurgated edition of the scriptures, you will need their interpretation. Who is the best interpreter? Not learned men surely. Learning there must be. But religion does not live by it. It lives in the experiences of its saints and seers, in their lives and sayings. When all the most learned commentators of the scriptures are utterly forgotten, the accumulated experience of the sages and saints will abide and be an inspiration for ages to come.

Caste has nothing to do with religion. It is a custom whose origin I do not know, and do not need to know for the satisfaction of my spiritual hunger. But I do know that it is harmful both to spiritual and national growth. Varna and ashrama are institutions which have nothing to do with castes. The law of varna teaches us that we have each one of us to earn our bread by following the ancestral calling. It defines not our rights but our duties. It necessarily has reference to callings that are conducive to the welfare of humanity and to no other. It also follows that there is no calling too low and none too high. All are good, lawful and absolutely equal in status. The callings of a Brahmin—spiritual teacher—and a scavenger are equal, and their due performance carries equal merit before God, and at one time seems to have carried identical reward before man. Both were entitled to their livelihood and no more. Indeed, one traces even now in the villages the faint lines of this healthy operation of the law.

Living in Segaon with its population of six hundred, I do not find a great disparity between the earnings of different tradesmen, including Brahmins. I find too that real Brahmins are to be found, even in these degenerate days, who are living on alms freely given to them and are giving freely of what they have of spiritual treasures. It would be wrong and improper to judge the law of varna by its caricature in the lives of men who profess to belong to a varna, whilst they openly commit a breach of its only operative rule. Arrogation of a superior status by and of a varna over another is a denial of the law. And there is nothing in the law of varna to warrant a belief in untouchability. (The essence of Hinduism is contained in its enunciation of one and only God as truth and its bold acceptance of ahimsa as the law of the human family.)

I am aware that my interpretation of Hinduism will be disputed by many besides Dr Ambedkar. That does not affect my position. It is an interpretation by which I have lived for nearly half a century, and according to which I have endeavoured to the best of my ability to regulate my life.

In my opinion the profound mistake that Dr Ambedkar has made in his address is to pick out the texts of doubtful authenticity and value, and the state of degraded Hindus who are no fit specimens of the faith they so woefully misrepresent.

Judged by the standard applied by Dr Ambedkar every known living faith will probably fail.

In his able address, the learned doctor has over-proved his case. Can a religion that was professed by Chaitanya, Jnyandeo, Tukaram, Tiruvalluvar, Ramakrishna Paramahansa, Raja Ram Mohan Roy, Maharshi Devendranath Tagore, Vivekananda, and a host of others who might be easily mentioned, be so utterly devoid of merit as is made out in Dr Ambedkar's address? A religion has to be judged not by its worst specimens but by the best it might have produced. For that and that alone can be used as the standard to aspire to, if not to improve upon.

Harijan, 18 July 1936

SANT RAM RESPONDS TO GANDHI

VARNA VERSUS CASTE

Shri Sant Ramji of the Jat-Pat Todak Mandal of Lahore wants me to publish the following:

"I have read your remarks about Dr Ambedkar and the Jat-Pat Todak Mandal, Lahore. In that connection I beg to submit as follows:

"We did not invite Dr Ambedkar to preside over our conference because he belonged to the Depressed Classes, for we do not distinguish between a Touchable and an Untouchable Hindu. On the contrary our choice fell on him simply because his diagnosis of the fatal disease of the Hindu community was the same as ours, i.e., he too was of the opinion that the caste system was the root cause of the disruption and downfall of the Hindus. The subject of the doctor's thesis for his doctorate being the caste system, he has studied the subject thoroughly. Now the object of our conference was to persuade the Hindus to annihilate caste, but the advice of a non-Hindu in social and religious matters can have no effect on them. The doctor in the supplementary portion of his address insisted on saying that that was his last speech as a Hindu, which was irrelevant as well as pernicious to the interests of the conference. So, we requested him to expunge that sentence, for he could easily say the same thing on any other occasion. But he refused, and we saw no utility in making merely a show of our function. In spite of all this, I cannot help praising his address, which is, as far as I know, the most learned thesis on the subject and worth translating into every vernacular of India.

Moreover, I want to bring to your notice that your philosophical difference between caste and varna is too subtle to be grasped by people in general, because for all practical purposes in Hindu society, caste and varna are one and the same thing, for the function of both of them is one and the same, i.e. to restrict inter-caste marriages and inter-dining. Your theory of varnavyavastha is impracticable in this age, and there is no hope of its revival in the near future. But Hindus are slaves of caste, and do not want to destroy it. So, when you advocate your ideal of imaginary varnavyavastha, they find justification for clinging to caste. Thus, you are doing a great disservice to social reform by advocating your imaginary utility of the division of varnas, for it creates a hindrance in our way. To try to remove untouchability without striking at the root of varnavyavastha is simply to treat the outward symptoms of a disease, or to draw a line on the surface of water. As in the heart of their hearts dwijas do not want to give social equality to the so-called Touchable and Untouchable Shudras, so they refuse to break caste—and give liberal donations for the removal of untouchability simply to evade the issue. To seek the help of the shastras for the removal of untouchability and caste is simply to wash mud with mud."

The last paragraph of the letter surely cancels the first. If the Mandal rejects the help of the shastras, they do exactly what Dr Ambedkar does, i.e., cease to be Hindus. How then can they object to Dr Ambedkar's address merely because he said that that was his last speech as a Hindu? The position appears to be wholly untenable, especially when the Mandal, for which Shri Sant Ram claims to speak, applauds the whole argument of Dr Ambedkar's address.

But it is pertinent to ask what the Mandal believes in, if it rejects the shastras. How can a Muslim remain one if he rejects the Quran, or a Christian remain Christian if he rejects the Bible? If caste and varna are convertible terms, and if varna is an integral part of the shastras which define Hinduism, I do not know how a person who rejects caste, i.e., varna, can call himself a Hindu.

Shri Sant Ram likens the shastras to mud. Dr Ambedkar has not, so far as I remember, given any such picturesque name to the shastras. I have certainly meant when I have said: that if shastras support the existing untouchability I should cease to call myself a Hindu. Similarly, if the shastras support caste, as we know it today in all its hideousness, I may not call myself or remain a Hindu, since I have no scruples about inter-dining or intermarriage. I need not repeat my position regarding shastras and their interpretation. I venture to suggest to Shri Sant Ram that it is the only rational and correct and morally defensible position, and it has ample warrant in Hindu tradition.

Harijan, 15 August 1936

A REPLY TO THE MAHATMA

B.R. Ambedkar

I appreciate greatly the honour done me by the Mahatma in taking notice in his *Harijan* of the speech on caste which I had prepared for the Jat-Pat Todak Mandal. From a perusal of his review of my speech, it is clear that the Mahatma completely dissents from the views I have expressed on the subject of caste. I am not in the habit of entering into controversy with my opponents unless there are special reasons which compel me to act otherwise. Had my opponent been some mean and obscure person I would not have pursued him. But my opponent being the Mahatma himself, I feel I must attempt to meet the case to the contrary which he has sought to put forth.

While I appreciate the honour he has done me, I must confess to a sense of surprise on finding that of all people the Mahatma should accuse me of a desire to seek publicity, as he seems to do when he suggests that in publishing the undelivered speech my object was to see that I was not 'forgotten'. Whatever the Mahatma may choose to say, my object in publishing the speech was to provoke the Hindus to think, and to take stock of their position. I have never hankered for publicity, and if I may say so, I have more of it than I wish or need. But supposing it was out of the motive of gaining publicity that I printed the speech, who could cast a stone at me? Surely not those who, like the Mahatma, live in glass houses.

Motive apart, what has the Mahatma to say on the question raised by me in the speech? First of all, anyone who reads my speech will realise that the Mahatma has entirely missed the issues raised by me, and that the issues he has raised are not the issues that arise out of what he is pleased to call my indictment of the Hindus. The principal points which I have tried to make out in my speech may be catalogued as follows:

(1) That caste has ruined the Hindus; (2) that the reorganisation of Hindu society on the basis of chaturvarnya is impossible because the varnavyavastha is like a leaky pot or like a man running at the nose. It is incapable of sustaining itself by its own virtue and has an inherent tendency to degenerate into

a caste system unless there is a legal sanction behind it which can be enforced against everyone transgressing his varna; (3) that the reorganisation of Hindu society on the basis of chaturvarnya would be harmful, because the effect of the varnavyavastha would be to degrade the masses by denying them opportunity to acquire knowledge and to emasculate them by denying them the right to be armed; (4) that Hindu society must be reorganised on a religious basis which would recognise the principles of liberty, equality and fraternity; (5) that in order to achieve this object the sense of religious sanctity behind caste and varna must be destroyed; (6) that the sanctity of caste and varna can be destroyed only by discarding the divine authority of the shastras.

It will be noticed that the questions raised by the Mahatma are absolutely besides the point, and show that the main argument of the speech was lost upon him.

Let me examine the substance of the points made by the Mahatma. The first point made by the Mahatma is that the texts cited by me are not authentic. I confess I am no authority on this matter. But I should like to state that the texts cited by me are all taken from the writings of the late Mr Tilak, who was a recognised authority on the Sanskrit language and on the Hindu shastras. His second point is that these shastras should be interpreted not by the learned but by the saints; and that as the saints have understood them the shastras do not support caste and untouchability.

As regards the first point, what I would like to ask the Mahatma is, what does it avail to anyone if the texts are interpolations, and if they have been differently interpreted by the saints? The masses do not make any distinction between texts which are genuine and texts which are interpolations. The masses do not know what the texts are. They are too illiterate to know the contents of the shastras. They have believed what they have been told, and what they have been told is that the shastras do enjoin as a religious duty the observance of caste and untouchability.

With regard to the saints, one must admit that howsoever different and elevating their teachings may have been as compared to those of the merely learned, they have been lamentably ineffective. They have been ineffective for two reasons. Firstly, none of the saints ever attacked the caste system. On the contrary—they were staunch believers in the system of castes. Most of them lived and died as members of the castes to which they respectively belonged. So passionately attached was Jnyandeo to his status as a Brahmin that when the Brahmins of Paithan would not admit him to their fold, he moved heaven and earth to get his status as a Brahmin recognised by the Brahmin fraternity.

And even the saint Eknath, who now figures in the film *Dharmatma* as a hero for having shown the courage to touch the Untouchables and dine with them, did so not because he was opposed to caste and untouchability, but because he felt that the pollution caused thereby could be washed away by a bath in the sacred waters of the river Ganges. The saints have never, according to my study, carried on a campaign against caste and untouchability. They were not concerned with the struggle between men. They were concerned with the relation between man and god. They did not preach that all men were equal. They preached that all men were equal in the eyes of god—a very different and a very innocuous proposition, which nobody can find difficult to preach or dangerous to believe in.

The second reason why the teachings of the saints proved ineffective was because the masses have been taught that a saint might break caste, but the common man must not. A saint therefore never became an example to follow. He always remained a pious man to be honoured. That the masses have remained staunch believers in caste and untouchability shows that the pious lives and noble sermons of the saints have had no effect on their life and conduct, as against the teachings of the shastras. Thus, it can be a matter of no consolation that there were saints, or that there is a Mahatma who understands the shastras differently from the learned few or ignorant many.

That the masses hold a different view of the shastras is a fact which should and must be reckoned with. How that is to be dealt with, except by denouncing the authority of the shastras which continue to govern their conduct, is a question which the Mahatma has not considered. But whatever the plan the Mahatma puts forth as an effective means to free the masses from the teachings of the shastras, he must accept that the pious life led by one good Samaritan may be very elevating to himself, but in India, with the attitude the common man has to saints and to Mahatmas—to honour but not to follow—one cannot make much out of it.

The third point made by the Mahatma is that a religion professed by Chaitanya, Jnyandeo, Tukaram, Tiruvalluvar, Ramakrishna Paramahansa, etc., cannot be devoid of merit as is made out by me, and that a religion has to be judged not by its worst specimens but by the best it might have produced. I agree with every word of this statement. But I do not quite understand what the Mahatma wishes to prove thereby. That religion should be judged not by its worst specimens but by its best is true enough, but does it dispose of the matter? I say it does not.

The question still remains, why the worst number so many and the best so few. To my mind there are two conceivable answers to this question: (1) that the worst by reason of some original perversity of theirs are morally uneducable, and are therefore incapable of making the remotest approach to the religious ideal. Or: (2) that the religious ideal is a wholly wrong ideal which has given a wrong moral twist to the lives of the many, and that the best have become best in spite of the wrong ideal—in fact, by giving to the wrong twist a turn in the right direction.

Of these two explanations I am not prepared to accept the first, and I am sure that even the Mahatma will not insist upon the contrary. To my mind the second is the only logical and reasonable explanation, unless the Mahatma has a third alternative to explain why the worst are so many and the best so few. If the second is the only explanation, then obviously the argument of the Mahatma that a religion should be judged by its best followers carries us nowhere—except to pity the lot of the many who have gone wrong because they have been made to worship wrong ideals.

The argument of the Mahatma that Hinduism would be tolerable if only many were to follow the example of the saints is fallacious for another reason. (In this connection, see the illuminating article on "Morality and the Social Structure" by H.N. Brailsford in the *Aryan Path* for April 1936.) By citing the names of such illustrious persons as Chaitanya, etc., what the Mahatma seems to me to suggest in its broadest and simplest form is that Hindu society can be made tolerable and even happy without any fundamental change in its structure, if all the high-caste Hindus can be persuaded to follow a high standard of morality in their dealings with the low-caste Hindus. I am totally opposed to this kind of ideology.

I can respect those of the caste Hindus who try to realise a high social ideal in their life. Without such men, India would be an uglier and a less happy place to live in than it is. But nonetheless, anyone who relies on an attempt to turn the members of the caste Hindus into better men by improving their personal character is, in my judgement, wasting his energy and hugging an illusion. Can personal character make the maker of armaments a good man, i.e., a man who will sell shells that will not burst and gas that will not poison? If it cannot, how can you accept personal character to make a man loaded with the consciousness of caste a good man, i.e., a man who would treat his fellow men as his friends and equals? To be true to himself he must deal with his fellow man either as a superior or inferior, according as the case may be; at any rate, differently from his own caste-fellows. He can never be expected to deal with his fellow men as his kinsmen and equals.

As a matter of fact, a Hindu does treat all those who are not of his caste as though they were aliens, who could be discriminated against with impunity, and against whom any fraud or trick may be practised without shame. This is to say that there can be a better or a worse Hindu. But a good Hindu there cannot be. This is so not because there is anything wrong with his personal character. In fact, what is wrong is the entire basis of his relationship to his fellows. The best of men cannot be moral if the basis of relationship between them and their fellows is fundamentally a wrong relationship. To a slave, his master may be better or worse. But there cannot be a good master. A good man cannot be a master, and a master cannot be a good man.

The same applies to the relationship between high caste and low caste. To a low-caste man, a high-caste man can be better or worse as compared to other high-caste men. A high-caste man cannot be a good man, in so far as he must have a low caste man to distinguish him as a high-caste man. It cannot be good to a low-caste man to be conscious that there is a high-caste man above him. I have argued in my speech that a society based on varna or caste is a society which is based on a wrong relationship. I had hoped that the Mahatma would attempt to demolish my argument. But instead of doing that, he has merely reiterated his belief in chaturvarnya without disclosing the ground on which it is based.

Does the Mahatma practise what he preaches? One does not like to make personal reference in an argument which is general in its application. But when one preaches a doctrine and holds it as a dogma there is a curiosity to know how far he practises what he preaches. It may be that his failure to practise is due to the ideal being too high to be attainable; it may be that his failure to practise is due to the innate hypocrisy of the man. In any case he exposes his conduct to examination, and I must not be blamed if I ask how far has the Mahatma attempted to realise his ideal in his own case?

The Mahatma is a Bania trader by birth. His ancestors had abandoned trading in favour of ministership, which is a calling of the Brahmins. In his own life, before he became a Mahatma, when the occasion came for him to choose his career he preferred law to scales. On abandoning law, he became half saint and half politician. He has never touched trading, which is his ancestral calling.

His youngest son—I take the one who is a faithful follower of his father—was born a Vaishya, has married a Brahmin's daughter, and has chosen to serve a newspaper magnate. The Mahatma is not known to have condemned him for not following his ancestral calling. It may be wrong and uncharitable to judge an ideal by its worst specimens. But surely the Mahatma as a specimen is no better, and if he even fails to realise the ideal then the ideal must be an impossible ideal, quite opposed to the practical instincts of man.

Students of Carlyle know that he often spoke on a subject before he thought about it. I wonder whether such has not been the case with the Mahatma in regard to the subject matter of caste. Otherwise, certain questions which occur to me would not have escaped him. When can a calling be deemed to have become an ancestral calling, so as to make it binding on a man? Must a man follow his ancestral calling even if it does not suit his capacities, even when it has ceased to be profitable? Must a man live by his ancestral calling even if he finds it to be immoral? If everyone must pursue his ancestral calling, then it must follow that a man must continue to be a pimp because his grandfather was a pimp, and a woman must continue to be a prostitute because her grandmother was a prostitute. Is the Mahatma prepared to accept the logical conclusion of his doctrine? To me his ideal of following one's ancestral calling is not only an impossible and impractical ideal, but it is also morally an indefensible ideal.

The Mahatma sees great virtue in a Brahmin remaining a Brahmin all his life. Leaving aside the fact that there are many Brahmins who do not like to remain Brahmins all their lives, what can we say about those Brahmins who have clung to their ancestral calling of priesthood? Do they do so from any faith in the virtue of the principle of ancestral calling, or do they do so from motives of filthy lucre? The Mahatma does not seem to concern himself with such queries. He is satisfied that these are "real Brahmins who are living on alms freely given to them, and giving freely what they have of spiritual treasures". This is how a hereditary Brahmin priest appears to the Mahatma— a carrier of spiritual treasures.

But another portrait of the hereditary Brahmin can also be drawn. A Brahmin can be a priest to Vishnu—the god of love. He can be a priest to Shankar—the god of destruction. He can be a priest at Buddha Gaya worshipping Buddha—the greatest teacher of mankind, who taught the noblest doctrine of love. He also can be a priest to Kali, the goddess who must have a daily sacrifice of an animal to satisfy her thirst for blood. He will be a priest of the temple of Rama—the Kshatriya god! He will also be a priest of the temple of Parshuram, the god who took on an avatar to destroy the Kshatriyas! He can be a priest to Brahma, the creator of the world. He can be a priest to a pir, whose god Allah will not brook the claim of Brahma to share his spiritual dominion over the world! No one can say that this is a picture which is not true to life.

If this is a true picture, one does not know what to say of this capacity to bear loyalties to gods and goddesses whose attributes are so antagonistic that no honest man can be a devotee to all of them. The Hindus rely upon this extraordinary phenomenon as evidence of the greatest virtue of their religion—namely, its catholicity, its spirit of toleration. As against this facile view, it can be urged that what is toleration and catholicity may be really nothing more creditable than indifference or flaccid latitudinarianism. These two attitudes are hard to distinguish in their outer seeming. But they are so vitally unlike in their real quality that no one who examines them closely can mistake one for the other.

That a man is ready to render homage to many gods and goddesses may be cited as evidence of his tolerant spirit. But can it not also be evidence of an insincerity born of a desire to serve the times? I am sure that this toleration is merely insincerity. If this view is well founded, one may ask, what spiritual treasure can there be within a person who is ready to be a priest and a devotee to any deity which it serves his purpose to worship and to adore? Not only must such a person be deemed to be bankrupt of all spiritual treasures, but for him to practise so elevating a profession as that of a priest simply because it is ancestral—without faith, without belief, merely as a mechanical process handed down from father to son—is not a conservation of virtue; it is really the prostitution of a noble profession which is no other than the service of religion.

Why does the Mahatma cling to the theory of everyone following his or her ancestral calling? He gives his reasons nowhere. But there must be some reason, although he does not care to avow it. Years ago, writing on "Caste versus Class" in his *Young India,* he argued that the caste system was better than a class system on the ground that caste was the best possible adjustment for social stability. If that be the reason why the Mahatma clings to the theory of everyone following his or her ancestral calling, then he is clinging to a false view of social life.

Everybody wants social stability, and some adjustment must be made in the relationship between individuals and classes in order that stability may be had. But two things, I am sure, nobody wants. One thing nobody wants is a static relationship, something that is unalterable, something that is fixed for all times. Stability is wanted, but not at the cost of change when change is imperative. The second thing nobody wants is mere adjustment. Adjustment is wanted, but not at the sacrifice of social justice.

Can it be said that the adjustment of social relationships on the basis of caste—i.e., on the basis of each to his hereditary calling— avoids these two evils? I am convinced that it does not. Far from being the best possible adjustment, I have no doubt that it is of the worst possible kind, inasmuch as it offends against both the canons of social adjustment—namely, fluidity and equity.

Some might think that the Mahatma has made much progress, inasmuch as he now only believes in varna and does not believe in caste. It is true that there was a time when the Mahatma was a full-blooded and a blue-blooded Sanatani Hindu. He believed in the Vedas, the Upanishads, the puranas, and all that goes by the name of Hindu scriptures; and therefore, in avatars and rebirth. He believed in caste and defended it with the vigour of the orthodox. He condemned the cry for inter-dining, inter-drinking, and intermarrying, and argued that restraints about inter-dining to a great extent "helped the cultivation of will-power and the conservation of a certain social virtue".

It is good that he has repudiated this sanctimonious nonsense and admitted that caste "is harmful both to spiritual and national growth", and maybe his son's marriage outside his caste has had something to do with this change of view. But has the Mahatma really progressed? What is the nature of the varna for which the Mahatma stands? Is it the Vedic conception as commonly understood and preached by Swami Dayanand Saraswati and his followers, the Arya Samajists?

The essence of the Vedic conception of varna is the pursuit of a calling which is appropriate to one's natural aptitude. The essence of the Mahatma's conception of varna is the pursuit of one's ancestral calling, irrespective of natural aptitude.

What is the difference between caste and varna, as understood by the Mahatma? I find none. As defined by the Mahatma varna becomes merely a different name for caste, for the simple reason that it is the same in essence—namely, pursuit of one's ancestral calling. Far from making progress, the Mahatma has suffered retrogression. By putting this interpretation upon the Vedic conception of varna, he has really made ridiculous what was sublime. While I reject the Vedic varnavyavastha for reasons given in the speech, I must admit that the Vedic theory of varna as interpreted by Swami Dayanand and some others is a sensible and an inoffensive thing. It did not admit birth as a determining factor in fixing the place of an individual in society. It only recognised worth.

The Mahatma's view of varna not only makes nonsense of the Vedic varna, but it makes it an abominable thing. Varna and caste are two very different concepts. Varna is based on the principle of each according to his worth, while caste is based on the principle of each according to his birth. The two are as distinct as chalk is from cheese. In fact, there is an antithesis between the two. If the Mahatma believes, as he does, in everyone following his or her ancestral calling, then most certainly he is advocating the caste system, and in calling it the varna system he is not only guilty of terminological inexactitude, but he is causing confusion worse confounded.

I am sure that all his confusion is due to the fact that the Mahatma has no definite and clear conception as to what is varna and what is caste, and as to the necessity of either for the conservation of Hinduism. He has said—and one hopes that he will not find some mystic reason to change his view—that caste is not the essence of Hinduism. Does he regard varna as the essence of Hinduism? One cannot as yet give any categorical answer.

Readers of his article on "Dr Ambedkar's Indictment" will answer "No." In that article he does not say that the dogma of varna is an essential part of the creed of Hinduism. Far from making varna the essence of Hinduism, he says "the essence of Hinduism is contained in its enunciation of one and only God as truth and its bold acceptance of ahimsa as the law of the human family".

But readers of his article in reply to Mr Sant Ram will say "Yes." In that article he says "How can a Muslim remain one if he rejects the Quran, or a Christian remain Christian if he rejects the Bible? If caste and varna are convertible terms, and if varna is an integral part of the shastras which define Hinduism, I do not know how a person who rejects caste, i.e., varna, can call himself a Hindu." Why this prevarication? Why does the Mahatma hedge?

Whom does he want to please? Has the saint failed to sense the truth? Or does the politician stand in the way of the saint?

The real reason why the Mahatma is suffering from this confusion is probably to be traced to two sources. The first is the temperament of the Mahatma. He has in almost everything the simplicity of the child, with the child's capacity for self-deception. Like a child, he can believe in anything he wants to believe in. We must therefore wait till such time as it pleases the Mahatma to abandon his faith in varna, as it has pleased him to abandon his faith in caste.

The second source of confusion is the double role which the Mahatma wants to play—of a Mahatma and a politician. As a Mahatma, he may be trying to spiritualise politics. Whether he has succeeded in it or not, politics have certainly commercialised him. A politician must know that society cannot bear the whole truth, and that he must not speak the whole truth; if he is speaking the whole truth it is bad for his politics. The reason why the Mahatma is always supporting caste and varna is because he is afraid that if he opposed them he would lose his place in politics. Whatever may be the source of this confusion the Mahatma must be told that he is deceiving himself, and also deceiving the people, by preaching caste under the name of varna.

The Mahatma says that the standards I have applied to test Hindus and Hinduism are too severe, and that judged by those standards every known living faith will probably fail. The complaint that my standards are high may be true. But the question is not whether they are high or whether they are low. The question is whether they are the right standards to apply. A people and their religion must be judged by social standards based on social ethics. No other standard would have any meaning, if religion is held to be a necessary good for the wellbeing of the people.

Now, I maintain that the standards I have applied to test Hindus and Hinduism are the most appropriate standards, and that I know of none that are better. The conclusion that every known religion would fail if tested by my standards may be true. But this fact should not give the Mahatma as the champion of Hindus and Hinduism a ground for comfort, any more than the existence of one madman should give comfort to another madman, or the existence of one criminal should give comfort to another criminal.

I would like to assure the Mahatma that it is not the mere failure of the Hindus and Hinduism which has produced in me the feelings of disgust and contempt with which I am charged. I realise that the world is a very imperfect world, and anyone who wants to live in it must bear with its imperfections.

But while I am prepared to bear with the imperfections and shortcomings of the society in which I may be destined to labour, I feel I should not consent to live in a society which cherishes wrong ideals, or a society which, having right ideals, will not consent to bring its social life into conformity with those ideals. If I am disgusted with Hindus and Hinduism, it is because I am convinced that they cherish wrong ideals and live a wrong social life. My quarrel with Hindus and Hinduism is not over the imperfections of their social conduct. It is much more fundamental. It is over their ideals.

Hindu society seems to me to stand in need of a moral regeneration which it is dangerous to postpone. And the question is, who can determine and control this moral regeneration? Obviously, only those who have undergone an intellectual regeneration and those who are honest enough to have the courage of their convictions born of intellectual emancipation. Judged by this standard, the Hindu leaders who count are, in my opinion, quite unfit for the task. It is impossible to say that they have undergone the preliminary intellectual regeneration. If they had undergone an intellectual regeneration, they would neither delude themselves in the simple way of the untaught multitude, nor would they take advantage of the primitive ignorance of others as one sees them doing.

Notwithstanding the crumbling state of Hindu society, these leaders will nevertheless unblushingly appeal to ideals of the past which have in every way ceased to have any connection with the present—ideals which, however suitable they might have been in the days of their origin, have now become a warning rather than a guide. They still have a mystic respect for the earlier forms which makes them disinclined—nay, opposed—to any examination of the foundations of their society. The Hindu masses are of course incredibly heedless in the formation of their beliefs. But so are the Hindu leaders. And what is worse is that these Hindu leaders become filled with an illicit passion for their beliefs when anyone proposes to rob them of their companionship.

The Mahatma is no exception. The Mahatma appears not to believe in thinking. He prefers to follow the saints. Like a conservative with his reverence for consecrated notions, he is afraid that if he once starts thinking, many ideals and institutions to which he clings will be doomed. One must sympathise with him. For every act of independent thinking puts some portion of an apparently stable world in peril.

But it is equally true that dependence on saints cannot lead us to know the truth. The saints are after all only human beings, and as Lord Balfour said, "the human mind is no more a truth-finding apparatus than the snout of a pig". In so far as he does think, to me he really appears to be prostituting his intelligence to find reasons for supporting this archaic social structure of the Hindus. He is the most influential apologist of it and therefore the worst enemy of the Hindus.

Unlike the Mahatma, there are Hindu leaders who are not content merely to believe and follow. They dare to think, and act in accordance with the result of their thinking. But unfortunately they are either a dishonest lot, or an indifferent lot when it comes to the question of giving right guidance to the mass of the people. Almost every Brahmin has transgressed the rule of caste. The number of Brahmins who sell shoes is far greater than those who practise priesthood. Not only have the Brahmins given up their ancestral calling of priesthood for trading, but they have entered trades which are prohibited to them by the shastras. Yet how many Brahmins who break caste every day will preach against caste and against the shastras?

For one honest Brahmin preaching against caste and shastras because his practical instinct and moral conscience cannot support a conviction in them, there are hundreds who bread caste and trample upon the shastras every day, but who are the most fanatic upholders of the theory of caste and the sanctity of the shastras. Why this duplicity? Because they feel that if the masses are emancipated from the yoke of caste, they would be a menace to the power and prestige of the Brahmins as a class. The dishonesty of this intellectual class, who would deny the masses the fruits of their thinking, is a most disgraceful phenomenon.

The Hindus, in the words of Matthew Arnold, are "wandering between two worlds, one dead, the other powerless to be born." What are they to do? The Mahatma to whom they appeal for guidance does not believe in thinking, and can therefore give no guidance which can be said to stand the test of experience. The intellectual classes to whom the masses look for guidance are either too dishonest or too indifferent to educate them in the right direction. We are indeed witnesses to a great tragedy. In the face of this tragedy all one can do is to lament and say—such are thy leaders, O Hindus!